IRAN'S NATIONAL SECURITY POLICY

CAPABILITIES, INTENTIONS & IMPACT

THE CARNEGIE ENDOWMENT FOR INTERNATIONAL PEACE

SHAHRAM CHUBIN

IRAN'S NATIONAL SECURITY POLICY:
INTENTIONS CAPABILITIES & IMPACT
BY SHAHRAM CHUBIN

A CARNEGIE
ENDOWMENT
BOOK

Copyright ©1994 by
THE CARNEGIE ENDOWMENT FOR INTERNATIONAL PEACE
2400 N Street, NW, Washington, D.C. 20037
All Rights Reserved

Library of Congress Cataloging-in-Publication data
Chubin, Shahram
Iran's national security policy: intentions,
capabilities, and impact / by Shahram Chubin
p. cm.
"A Carnegie Endowment book."
Includes index.

ISBN 0-87003-031-0 (pbk.) : $10.95
1. Iran—Foreign relations—1979- 2. National
security—Iran.
I. Title
DS318.83.C48 1993
327.55—dc20   93-43458
                              CIP

CARNEGIE
ENDOWMENT FOR
INTERNATIONAL
PEACE

The Carnegie Endowment was founded in 1910 by Andrew Carnegie to promote international peace and understanding. To that end the Endowment conducts programs of research, discussion, publication and education in international affairs and American foreign policy. The Endowment also publishes the quarterly journal *Foreign Policy*.

As a tax-exempt operating foundation, the Endowment maintains a professional staff of Senior and Resident Associates who bring to their work substantial firsthand experience in foreign affairs. Through writing, public and media appearances, Congressional testimony, participation in conferences, and other activities, the staff engages the major policy issues of the day in ways that reach both expert and general audiences. Accordingly the Endowment seeks to provide a hospitable umbrella under which responsible analysis and debate may be conducted, and it encourages Associates to write and speak freely on the subjects of their work. The Endowment convenes special policy forums and, from time to time, issues reports of commissions or study groups.

The Endowment normally does not take institutional positions on public policy issues. It supports its activities principally from its own resources, supplemented by non-governmental, philanthropic grants.

ACKNOWLEDGMENTS

I am indebted to numerous individuals for sharing their ideas and impressions with me. I would like to single out particularly the participants at the workshop on Iran in Castelgandolfo which was sponsored by ENI, Italy and organized by the Deutsches Orient-Institut, Hamburg in July 1992. Without the benefit of discussions over several sessions in the Study Group on Iran sponsored and convened by the Carnegie Endowment in 1992, this study would have been much the poorer.

The assistance and diligence of Jeremy Pressman in the preparation of the maps, charts as well as in miscellaneous research, has been especially helpful and has enhanced the final project for which I am grateful. In the various drafts I benefitted from the able and untiring efforts of Maria Alunan and Christine Bicknell who deciphered my handwriting and converted it into readable typescript. Thanks also go to Rebecca Krafft for her helpful and capable copyediting.

The entire production process at Carnegie has been a model of efficiency especially for an author located at some distance from the base. Copyediting and footnote checking have taken time but added, one hopes, to the quality of the final product. For substantive comments on the monograph I am indebted to Shaul Bakhash, Michael Eisenstadt and Richard Haass who shared with me their expertise.

For his counsel, practical assistance and encouragement I am especially grateful to Geoffrey Kemp. This work would not have been completed without his support. However for the interpretations offered and the limitations of this work, I alone am responsible.

SHAHRAM CHUBIN
Geneva

FOREWORD

In July 1988 Iran sued for peace in its brutal eight year war with Iraq. It was a humiliating moment, the more so because in the early days of the conflict Iran had won a number of impressive battles and had pushed the Iraqi invaders back across the Shatt al-Arab. These victories were squandered in a foolish offensive to invade Iraq with the purpose of overthrowing the Saddam Hussein regime and eventually the Arab monarchies of the Gulf. Once this policy was adopted, Iran became a pariah throughout most of the Arab world and in the West. Two principal factors contributed to Iran's military defeat: Ayatollah Khomeini's mistaken belief that infantry tactics based on human wave assaults by teenagers armed with the Koran could overwhelm the well equipped Iraqi heretics and the international arms embargo against Iran orchestrated by the United States which was particularly successful in crippling Iran's air power.

Two and a half years later Iran witnessed Iraq's precipitous reversal of fortune as allied air and ground forces defeated Saddam Hussein's victorious army in a matter of weeks. Yet the allied victory was a hardly a moment for Iran to savor; it demonstrated with brutal clarity the comparative weaknesses of the regime's much reduced military forces. It was therefore inevitable that Iran would embark on a rearmament program and seek, at the same time, to minimize the impact of future embargoes by diversifying its sources of new weapons and increasing its indigenous capacity to produce arms. Another, more ominous lesson is that Iran, like other radical but weak countries, may now see the cost-benefit advantages of weapons of mass destruction and adopt a multifaceted program to develop its own nuclear weapons.

Because Iran is such an important player in the Persian Gulf and because the United States has committed itself to the security of its Arab allies, no political settlement of Gulf conflicts, let alone arms control initiatives, are possible so long as these two countries remain enemies. For this reason the Carnegie Endowment's Project on Middle East Arms Control thought it important to undertake an objective and thorough study of Iran's security requirements, the nature and pace of the current Iranian rearmament program and the threats these developments pose for regional security.

Shahram Chubin is a distinguished Iranian scholar and former Director for Regional Security Studies at London's International Institute for Strategic Studies. He brings to the task a well established reputation as a fair but forceful critic and interpreter of the arcane world of Tehran politics and strategy. Chubin argues that the regime "remains hostile to the

United States and its allies and unreconciled to the current international order." Furthermore "Iran retains a capacity to act as a spoiler and irritant in a region of endemic instability..." However Chubin makes a persuasive case for not exaggerating the impact of the current Iranian military buildup. He writes that "Iran's military arsenal, even when anticipated deliveries are counted, remains smaller than it was at the beginning of the revolution." While correctly highlighting the uncertainties and dangers concerning Iran's nuclear program, Chubin believes that "Iran's conventional arms program commands more attention than its operational capacities warrant." Chubin's study adds immeasurably to our knowledge and understanding of one of the most vexing strategic issues in the Middle East.

GEOFFREY KEMP
Director, Middle East Arms Control Project
Carnegie Endowment for International Peace

TABLES AND FIGURES

To fit in with the change of events words, too, had to change their usual meanings. What used to be described as a thoughtless act of aggression was now regarded as the courage of a party member; to think of the future was merely another way of saying one was a coward; any idea of moderation was just an attempt to disguise one's unmanly character; ability to understand a question from all sides meant that one was totally unfitted for action. Fanatical enthusiasm was the mark of a real man, and to plot against an enemy behind his back was perfectly legitimate self-defense. Anyone who held violent opinions could always be trusted, and anyone who objected to them became suspect. To plot successfully was a sign of intelligence...and indeed most people are more ready to call villainy cleverness than simpleminded honesty. They are proud of the first quality and ashamed of the second.

THUCYDIDES
The Peloponnesian War, book three

The dilemma for successive generations of those politicians who graduated from oratory to administration was that they owed their own power to precisely the kind of rhetoric that made their own subsequent governance impossible. The Revolution as an insurrection would have been impossible without regular infusions of spleen and blood, but the Revolution as government was impossible unless they could be selectively managed.

SIMON SCHAMA
Citizens: A Chronicle of the French Revolution

INTRODUCTION

With the end of the cold war, two international threats have become more prominent: the proliferation of the weapons of mass destruction in the Third World and the emergence of a virulent strain of Islamic anti-Western militance, frequently referred to as "Islamic fundamentalism." Since its inception in 1979, the Islamic Republic of Iran, a self-proclaimed revolutionary state, has trumpeted its anti-Western rhetoric and its support for forces opposed to the West and the United States. It fought a long and costly war with its neighbor Iraq and witnessed the quick and decisive defeat of the same enemy by allied forces during the Gulf War. Iran is now embarked upon a program of defense modernization that encompasses weapons of mass destruction and missiles, while continuing to preach a radical ideology. An assessment of precisely how dangerous a threat Iran is to Persian Gulf oil supplies and other U.S. interests in the Middle East is urgently needed.

The Iranian regime is not easy to understand. There is a gap between its rhetoric and its actions; between its sense of grievance and its inflammatory behavior; and between its ideological and national interests. Nor are its actions consistent. However, it remains hostile to the United States and its allies and unreconciled to the current international order. It has not renounced its revolutionary aims and it continues to support international terrorism. Its ideology remains a potent motive force, and it seeks to exploit weakness where it can— locally in the Persian Gulf, regionally in the wider Middle East as well as farther afield.

In many respects the Islamic Republic has little to commend itself to others either as a model for revolution or as a strategic ally. However Iran retains a capacity to act as a spoiler and irritant in a region of endemic instability full of opportunities for subversion and intimidation. For this reason alone, Iran's military programs require examination. Their scope and pace, if sustained, could pose a threat to regional and Western interests. Development of certain conventional capabilities could cause problems for the United States and its allies. Of even greater concern, however, are the unanswered questions about the scope of Iran's nonconventional weapons programs and its intentions for them. Drawing inferences of intentions from procurement and acquisition policies can be misleading, but such a method of analysis also raises legitimate doubts as to the dangers Iran's possession of chemical, biological and nuclear capabilities and missile delivery systems poses locally, regionally and internationally.

This book seeks to define Iran's national security policy based on its relevant experience and assess its implications. These serve as the context and the conditioning factors underlying its military programs. Chapter one outlines the strategic environment from Iran's perspective. The experience of Iran's revolutionary regime over the past fifteen years is discussed in chapter two, and the political and military lessons derived from its wartime experience are set forth. Chapter three casts Iran's military procurement policy and programs in light of the lessons of experience. Chapter four evaluates the realistic threats Iran's arms programs pose to regional and international security followed in chapter five by a discussion of how Iran arrives at national security decisions. The concluding section considers Iran's domestic economic base and the constraints this imposes on its leadership. It also identifies a different order of threat, with far-reaching ramifications, from Iran's arms buildup—that of escalating a regional Middle Eastern arms race to encompass nonconventional means, with all the attendant risks of accident or preemptive strike that proliferation implies.

IRAN'S SECURITY PERSPECTIVES: LOCAL, REGIONAL AND INTERNATIONAL

The end of the cold war has neither increased Iran's security nor improved its international standing. Viewed from Iran the new international environment is a hostile one; the United States has emerged as the primary actor, unchecked and unbalanced, and pursuing its interests unopposed. The new system leaves weaker states with reduced leverage, increased fragmentation and less ability to organize in alliances such as the nonaligned movement. Yet such new dimensions of power as economic competitiveness threaten to render poorer states less important as well. Restive populations increasingly seek more accountable and representative leadership including better economic and political performance by their governments among their standard demands. The cold war no longer promises a guarantee of support for dictators, determining alignments, foreign aid or diplomatic support.

Iran is poorly equipped to maneuver in the new environment. Its loss of strategic leverage is compounded by its economic weakness and poor relations with the new dominant power, the United States. Its few friends are marginal states, Syria and Pakistan, for instance, and they have adjusted by seeking to accommodate the new order or to accept further isolation. With few exceptions its borders are unstable.

Viewed from Tehran, an arc of crisis stretches from Iraq in the west through the Kurdish region to the Transcaucasus and eastward to Tajikistan and Afghanistan. Threatening them all is the potential fragmentation of existing states, whether Iraq, Azerbaijan, Tajikistan or Afghanistan. Iran's security would be jeopardized by the disintegration of any one of these, for Iran is a polyglot empire in which more than 50 percent of the population is either non-Persian speaking or non-Shi'i. In the case of Kurdish restiveness in Iraq spilling over into Iran and Turkey, a clash between Tehran and Ankara could ensue.[1]

From Iran's perspective the situation in the south is not much better. Two wars in the Persian Gulf have consolidated U.S. ties with the Arab states and increased the U.S. military presence there.[2] This dilutes Tehran's inherent regional influence stemming from its demographic strengths, geographic advantages and (in the 1970s) military and economic predominance.

Above all, Iran now feels more vulnerable to U.S. might. The United States remains a hostile adversary, seeking to undo the regime and contain its Islamic revolutionary message. In its view, the United States is seeking hegemony over the Middle East directly and through such clients as Israel and such dependents as Saudi Arabia, which practice what it derisively terms "American Islam." Iran sees the United States behind ef-

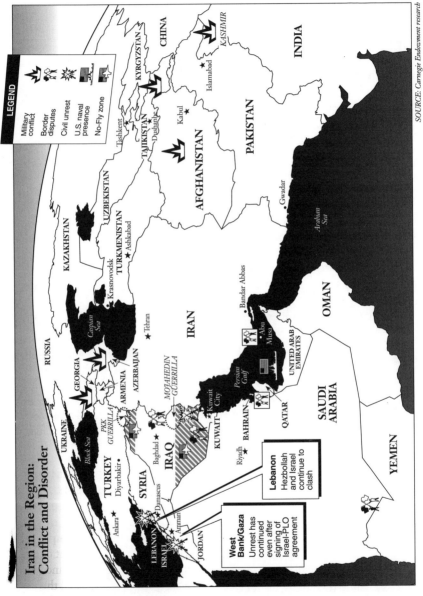

Iran in the Region:
Conflict and Disorder

LEGEND

Military conflict
Border disputes
Civil unrest
U.S. naval presence
No-Fly zone

West Bank/Gaza
Unrest has continued even after signing of Israel-PLO agreement

Lebanon
Hezbollah and Israel continue to clash

SOURCE: Carnegie Endowment research

forts in the north and south to encircle it militarily. Secretary of State James Baker, on his first visit to Central Asia in February 1992, admitted that a prime motivation behind U.S. policy there was the need to counter Iran. In the Gulf, Iran regards Arab efforts to set up a regional security arrangement that excludes it as a move guided by the United States to bar any Iranian role in regional politics. Iran in turn sees no room for the United States in the region and seeks to weaken its allies. It considers efforts to keep Iran artificially separate from the Gulf states as running counter to article 8 of U.N. Security Council resolution 598 (July 1987) which explicitly tied a cease-fire ending the Iran-Iraq War to movement toward a regional security arrangement.

Iran's antipathy toward the United States stems not only from regional politics. Iran attempts to advance Islam as one of its foreign policy goals. As the standard-bearer of Islam, Iran sees itself as inevitably opposed to the corrupt and unjust international system which an "arrogant" United States benefits from and upholds. Thus the emergence of the United States as the sole superpower confronts Iran with genuine problems that admit no clear solutions. The United States has proved that it can fashion an international coalition, obtain U.N. sanctions and devastate a neighboring country (Iraq) while suffering few casualties. Iran is keenly aware that the next military operation in the Middle East could be against its own forces. Yet it was unable to detect or respond effectively to the flights of U.S. missiles over Iranian territory during Desert Storm—not a reassuring circumstance.[3] In the aftermath of the war, the United States's establishment of "exclusion zones," which limit Iraq's sovereignty, appears to be a deliberate attempt at dismantling Iraq—a precedent Iran views with alarm.[4] In the meantime, a senior U.S. official articulated in May 1993 a "dual containment" policy that appears to equate Iran with Iraq and threatens to impede Iran's economic development.

Hostile relations with the United States create considerable difficulties for Iran: encirclement in the north and south, military threat, and economic or at least technological strangulation keeping the country backward. The tightening of unilateral U.S. controls on trade with and exports to Iran has increased by stages: first as a result of the Iran-Iraq War, then in response to Iranian terrorism and more recently on account of evidence concerning Iran's pursuit of technology related to missiles and weapons of mass destruction. In addition the United States has led the world powers to form multilateral suppliers' groups such as the Nuclear Supplier Club and the Missile Technology Control Regime, with stringent criteria for the transfer of technology. In defining "dual-use" technologies the United States is attempting to convince its allies in Europe and Asia and through the G-7 nations to restrict many categories of technology transfer to Iran.

The United States is using other means to cut off Iran as well. It has pressured the World Bank not to extend credits to Iran. On three occasions since 1991 it has publicized arms deliveries (missiles and chemical precursors) destined for Iran from North Korea or China, leaving an unspoken but implicit threat to intercept them.[5] U.S. pressure on India, Argentina and Pakistan has slowed Iran's access to nuclear technology. Tehran does not doubt given the enhanced weight of the United States and its own relative lack of importance, that equivalent U.S. pressure on Russia, North Korea or even China could deprive it of access to weapons technology (for no country values a relationship with Iran over one with the United States). U.S. intelligence will be the principal vehicle for monitoring arms control agreements, whether through the special inspections of the International Atomic Energy Agency for nuclear materials or those called for in the Chemical Weapons Convention; in both cases the United States has considerable and unique potential for making life difficult for Tehran. Quite apart from direct military threats, the United States can impose crippling burdens on Iran's economic and technological development. In short, from Tehran's perspective, the costs of hostility toward the United States have gone up in the post-cold war strategic environment.

RUSSIA AND THE NEW NORTH

The strategic benefits of the disintegration of a threatening and often belligerent USSR have been offset for Iran by disorder on its northern frontiers. The states of Iran's new north are politically unstable, at odds with their neighbors and erratic and uncertain in their orientation. Besides the possibility of getting entangled in their disputes with each another, Iran is concerned about ethnic conflicts like that between the Azeris and Armenians over the Nagorno-Karabakh region, which could spill over into Iran's own territory and pit its minorities against each other. In the case of the Tajik civil war, the Islamic opposition asked for Tehran's assistance. Iran's concern for the only Persian-speaking Central Asian state, reinforced by ideological affinities, had to be balanced by the pragmatic consideration that Iran could not afford to antagonize Russia, which supported the communist-led government. In the Transcaucasus, both involvement and noninvolvement hold risks for Iran. In January 1990 Iran supported the Azeris rhetorically against the Gorbachev government, denouncing their repression but without providing concrete assistance. In the Azeri conflict with the Armenians, Tehran has cultivated both sides because of its own Azeri populace. It has balanced a concern for the Azeris, its Shi'i but Turkic-speaking neighbors, with an interest in not encouraging Azeri extremism or a Muslim-Christian conflict. In the latest round of fighting in late 1993, Iran has sought to limit Armenian military gains and to discourage Azeri refugees from fleeing into Iranian Azerbaijan, where they could be politically destabilizing.

While the breakup of the USSR with its 50 million Muslims, is often depicted as fertile territory for Islamic activism, Iran has considerable practical constraints against interfering: minorities, border security and resource limitations have prompted Iran not to take sides or to offer much assistance. An inclination to capitalize on religious ties (especially with Azerbaijan) or cultural ties (as with Tajikistan) certainly exists in Iran. But instability and divisions within these states impose practical limitations.

Iran's top priority in the north remains its relations with Russia, limiting its freedom to maneuver in the region. Russia is important to Iran as a source of technology and arms, a prospective diplomatic partner and a counterweight of sorts to the United States. Iran and Russia are bound to interact in the Transcaucasus, Central Asia and the Persian Gulf. The nature of that interaction is still unfolding and depends heavily on the evolution of politics in Russia and the region. Iran, which is not represented diplomatically in the Conference on Security and Cooperation in Europe (CSCE) or its so-called Minsk Group (countries designed to initiate discussions about Nagorno-Karabakh), has every incentive to keep Moscow from joining an anti-Iranian Western coalition.

Iran's leverage is limited given the importance Moscow assigns its relations with Washington. Moreover some Russian factions, mainly in the military, are using the "threat from the south" (usually depicted as Islamic radicalism) as the rationale for a new mission for a rapidly deployable military. At the very least, Russia's sensitivity to the security of its frontiers and any intrusion by foreign powers into bordering nations (the independent Muslim republics), offset by Iran's potential as an export market for arms among other things, makes Iran an object of serious scrutiny.

All this tends to inhibit the emergence of clear parameters for Iranian diplomacy. Russian warnings influenced Iran to avoid becoming involved in Tajikistan (though the distance between the countries may also have been a factor).[6] Russian expressions of concern over Iranian troop deployments near the Russian-Azerbaijan border in August 1993 were also clearly heeded.[7] Iran benefits, however, from Russia's interest in cultivating a belt of friendly states on its borders, and it gains a certain advantage from Moscow's suspicions about Turkey's intentions. If the price of good relations and access to Russian arms supplies is Iranian restraint on its northern frontiers, since June 1989, when President Hashemi Rafsanjani visited Moscow (and Baku), Iran has signaled that the price is acceptable. In its restraint toward Azerbaijan the following year and in its reaction to the disintegration of the USSR in autumn of 1991, Iran demonstrated a singular lack of enthusiasm for activism. This need to cultivate Russian goodwill will tend to reinforce Iranian conservatism toward territorial issues stemming from the possible disintegration of neighboring states.

TURKEY: SECULAR NEIGHBOR

Iran's perspective on Turkey is influenced by concerns for political security and ideology. Turkey is a member of NATO and the permission it gave its allies, especially the United States, to use its airfields for military contingencies in Desert Storm could well recur. Second, Turkey is the only secular Islamic state, therefore it represents a threat to the Islamic model. Turkey poses no immediate danger to Iran, but it is a challenge.

The two countries have no territorial disputes; their relations over the past fifty years have largely been devoid of tension except over Iranian-sponsored terrorism. This situation may end with the new fluidity of the post-cold war period. Historical rivalries between the Ottoman and Safavid empires may be revived especially in the Transcaucasus. Stubborn regimes, inept diplomacy and clumsy strategy may lead to both countries' entanglement in regional disputes. Events that Iran may construe as Turkish political activism in Central Asia may stimulate a competitive impulse in Tehran and give rise to a more hostile rivalry. Such a development is possible and unpredictable. The evidence to date indicates an attitude of caution on both sides; Tehran does not rate competition with Turkey high among its security priorities and vice versa.

What concerns Tehran more is that Turkey may become an instrument of U.S. diplomacy in the region, either in the Persian Gulf or in Central Asia. Iran closely observes the modernization of the Turkish military and the possible use of its military installations. Especially in northern Gulf contingencies, Turkey could play an important role in support of U.S. aims; Iran would, of course, consider this a hostile action.

For Iranians this potential security problem has no obvious solution. Bilateral relations with Ankara remain correct; a border security agreement has been concluded and regular foreign ministerial-level meetings (which include Syria) have been instituted to address Iraq and the Kurdish question. Beneath the formal relations, however, tensions remain. Ankara accuses Tehran of supporting the separatist PKK (the Marxist-leaning Kurdish Workers' Party) which has waged a bloody decade-long guerrilla war in southeast Turkey. It also suspects elements within Iran of hiring and training terrorists for attacks on Turkish and Iranian targets, including two assassinations of prominent secularists and journalists in 1993 and possibly others. Iran is also believed to fund extremist elements within Turkey.

Iran counters with accusations that Turkey is providing sanctuary for the Mojahedin opponents of the Islamic Republic. This suspicion may motivate Tehran's support for the PKK, for Iran has no other interest in the Marxist group. But it does not explain the apparent pattern of terrorist attacks on Turkish, Israeli and U.S. targets in Turkey over the past decade by Islamic Jihad or other Iranian-supported groups. Turkey is aware of Iran's involvement in terrorism but has been reluctant to make this the basis of an outright breach between the neighboring states.

Iran's terrorist attacks and the disturbances it has incited (most recently over the Salman Rushdie issue) are usually seen as an effort to undermine secular government (that is, based on ideological grounds). They are also consistent with the Islamic Republic's tendency to engage in quid pro quo tactics (as in the 1992 bombing of the Israeli embassy in Buenos Aires in retaliation for the killing of the Hezbollah leader Moussavi). Finally, they reflect a determination to gain leverage over a neighbor or to inhibit certain Turkish policies, for instance, too close an alliance with the United States. Iran's subversion is both an attempt to undermine these ties and to divide Turkish society, in order to replace its secular government with one more congenial to Iran's world view.

THE PERSIAN GULF: AN ECONOMIC AND SECURITY BALANCE

Iran's strategic importance has been magnified by the temporary absence of Iraq from Persian Gulf politics. Two military interventions in the Gulf by foreign powers in five years (1987 and 1990-91) have heightened Iran's sense of vulnerability. The Arab states of the Persian Gulf, no longer inhibited, have established more concrete security relationships with the United States, and they have undergone qualitative military buildups, with U.S. assistance. Recent events—the Iran-Iraq War, Iran's revolutionary activities and its past claims on its neighbors—have intensified the sectarian, national and political rifts between Persian and Arab, Shi'i and Sunni. Iran seeks to organize regional security without outside powers, but its Arab neighbors have concluded that there can be no security without them.[8]

Iran's defense buildup has been viewed with alarm by other Gulf states. They tend to view Iran—revolutionary or not—as a threat to their security because of its great size and the presence of Shi'i minorities in several Gulf states, notably Kuwait, Bahrain and Saudi Arabia. Iran's attempts to improve its relations with these states are thus impeded in part by its size and geography, and limited as well by recent events—the memory of the 1980s and the ambiguity of Iranian policies combining reassurances with attempts at subversion or domination.[9] The result is a propensity on the part of these states, led by Saudi Arabia, to conclude security arrangements without reference to Iran (or Iraq).

The concerns Iran voices for security in the Persian Gulf are not simply rhetorical. Unlike other oil producers, who have access to overland routes, all Iran's oil exports go through the waterway. These exports account for more than 95 percent of its foreign exchange revenues, which enable it to import food for its exploding population and undertake the reconstruction of the country. Freedom of navigation is a survival issue for Iran, and throughout the war (1980-88) it sought to prevent Iraq or other states from denying it.

Relations with its Gulf neighbors are heavily influenced by Iran's dependence on oil exports, leaving it vulnerable in the extreme to price fluctuations. Oil prices have been weak since 1986, with revenues unstable and declining. In terms of purchasing power, oil prices in mid-1993 were lower than they were twenty years before.[10] Thus Iran, whose population in that period has doubled to 60 million, has more mouths to feed and lower oil income (roughly $15 billion a year versus $23 billion in 1983). Iran depends on keeping oil prices as high as possible and on maintaining some form of price stability within an OPEC cartel capable of influencing if not dictating prices. In these areas, Iran relies on solidarity within OPEC and on the actions of its most important member, Saudi Arabia.

Saudi Arabia, with its production capacity of some 9 million barrels a day, can dominate prices inside or outside OPEC. In 1986 it flooded the market and depressed oil prices, damaging Iran's war effort. Today, if it wished, it could reduce production and strengthen prices. Above all it can decide whether to accommodate the return of Kuwait and Iraq to the oil market by reducing its own production or ask, as it has, for cutbacks in the cartel members' quotas based on production capacity. Iran, which wants as large a quota as possible, anxiously supports cutbacks based on historical quotas rather than production capacity. Saudi Arabia remains the key player in this area, which is critically important for Iran's economic security.

This is not to say that Iran sees its security only in defensive or economic terms. It will certainly continue to try to spread its populist message and capitalize on local discontent. Political instability in the Arabian Peninsula may become more likely in a decade of relative economic austerity and as political consciousness grows.[11] Divisions among the Arab states over territorial, dynastic or succession disputes may also supply Iran with the political openings it needs. As of late 1993, these Arab states seem insulated against potential Iranian charges of being American lackeys, but their circumstances could change depending on economic performance. As in the past, Iran will seek to normalize ties while cultivating and maintaining its options for subversion and agitation. It has other interests in the balance as well, however: to keep from deepening the rift with its neighbors, intensifying its own isolation, and to maintain workable relations with Saudi Arabia.

Relations with key states and security in the Persian Gulf are thus central to Iranian interests. The same is true with Iraq. In the short term international ostracism of Iraq serves Iran's interest: Baghdad remains weak—a pariah unable to export oil—leaving Iran free to rebuild its military, mend fences in the Persian Gulf and keep its oil quota as high as possible. If a more moderate regime came to power in Iraq these advantages would end. Competition in Gulf diplomacy over oil exports would increase the strain on an already divided OPEC. Moreover, without Saddam Hussein Iraq could rise again to become a military threat (the Iran-Iraq cease-fire of August 1988 has never been formalized by a peace treaty). From such a vantage Iraq, particularly without Saddam, might play the "Arab card" to reintegrate itself into Persian Gulf politics, gesturing to the alleged Iranian threat and offering its smaller neighbors protection. A post-Saddam Iraqi regime might be more representative of society, granting Iraqi Shi'i (55 percent of the population) more power. Iran has shown few concrete indications of enthusiasm for the emergence of such a regime, possibly out of fear that it might represent a competitor.[12] Neither has Iran evinced any support for the fragmentation of Iraq: apart from the fact that Kurdish separatism in Iraq could spill over among Iran's Kurdish population (10 percent of the populace) encouraging demands for autonomy or even independence, there is the already-mentioned grave concern about the precedent it would set for the dismantling of purported "failed" states.

REVOLUTIONARY STANCES: SYMBOLISM AND SOLIDARITY

Iran's identity as a revolutionary Islamic state that is Shi'i (a minority comprising some 15 percent of the Muslim world) complicates its efforts to gain credibility and transcend the sectarian rift. Its leaders are compelled to stake out positions on Muslim issues internationally.[13] Iran has consistently argued that the only viable basis for cooperation among states is along the "Islamic axis." This article of faith has withstood the fragmentation of the Islamic world and two wars in the Persian Gulf between Muslim states. Iran sees the Islamic world's divisions together with deviation by some states from true Islam as the root cause of its failures. States that are subservient to the United States and abet its designs to weaken Islam are traitors to be eliminated.

Iran considers its own role in reviving Islam as central; its revolution is not just a national phenomenon, it is the "knell of awakening for the Muslim nations."[14] Iran's leaders depict their struggle as simultaneously combatting a corrupt monarchy and its foreign supporters and delivering "a slap in the face of arrogance." Much of their discourse, owing to their Shi'i sources, reflects a strong sense of grievance with an emphasis on tireless effort, resistance, striving, sacrifice and martyrdom. Even, perhaps especially, as underdog, Islamic Iran adheres resolutely to its principles.[15]

Revolutionary states commonly consider themselves as trail blazers and rarely settle for conventional foreign policies. This is in keeping with the assertion of Iran's spiritual leader Rahbar Khamenei that: "the [oppressed Muslim] nations need a role model to see that it is possible to stand firm against global arrogance. This role model is Islamic Iran."[16] Iran's leaders see a need to keep the spark of revolution alive, to keep the people mobilized and aware, as in a statement of Khamenei's that "The Islamic revolution is like a permanent volcano and the revolution continues to be alive."[17] Khamenei also states that other nations need not adopt Iran's structures but they should imitate its *attitude:* "steadfast, unyielding, uncompromising, an inflexible spirit in the face of global power and world domination."[18]

Iran's self-image as an embattled state adhering to the purest of principles in the face of superior powers awash in a sea of blasphemy and injustice, serves various functions and entails certain responsibilities. As Khamenei puts it, Iranian leaders "regard the defence of all Muslims in the world and Islamic sanctities everywhere as being among the great tasks of our great mission."[19] Iran's determination to play a broad and active international role is evident from the four hundred hours of foreign broadcasting in eighteen languages it produces each week, figures exceeded only by Egypt and India among developing countries.[20] At the same time, Iran's ambitions and claims make it susceptible to flattery by those who invoke Iran's model as a source of inspiration and make it difficult to reject requests for assistance.[21] It thus gets involved internationally because of its reputation as well as out of impulse.

Foremost among the responsibilities stemming from its self-proclaimed status as pathfinder and model is solidarity with oppressed Muslims everywhere. This is a core value of the revolution rather than a vital security interest, but it is an important part of Islamic Iran's sense of legitimacy and one of the few areas in which the regime can claim to be principled and unique. Iran repeatedly emphasizes its presence in areas where Muslim interests are at stake—from London and Bosnia to Algeria, Sudan, Palestine, Lebanon, Afghanistan and India (Kashmir). In each place Iran has engaged in some form of involvement. (Usually this has complicated its relations with some or several states; witness how its utterances on Kashmir have put a damper on relations with India.)

In every case part of Iran's motive has been to outbid other Islamic states, demonstrating Iran's capacity for self-sacrifice. This has been costly on several fronts: in relations with the West in the Salman Rushdie case; in relations with states in the region (such as Egypt) for its support to Sudan; and in the opening it gives other states to accuse Iran of meddling in their internal affairs and of masterminding a subversive international Islamic opposition. (Egypt's and Algeria's accusations, based on vast exaggerations of the role of foreign intervention in their own domestic problems are examples of this last.) Some of Iran's stances are pure posturing, such as the offer of 10,000 troops for a U.N. peacekeeping force for Bosnia. Others reflect genuine concern for Muslims, as in Iran's assistance to Afghanistan throughout the 1980s. Some issues, such as the *fatwa* against Rushdie, the burning of a mosque in India or the suppression of Muslim opposition in Algeria, reflect various motives: the determination to play a leadership role, the willingness to speak up at whatever cost, genuine concern about the issue and the desire to upstage other Muslim states (for instance Saudi Arabia).

ISRAEL/PALESTINE: A FOREIGN POLICY OR SECURITY ISSUE?

No cause has greater symbolic appeal in the Islamic world than the plight of the Palestinians, hence it is an issue that can be considered a gauge of leadership. Iranian leaders see it as an Islamic issue, giving them a right to be involved.[22] When framed as a Muslim rather than Arab issue, it provides a point of entry for Iran into the wider Middle East. Iran can argue that the tragedy of Palestine stems from the failure of regimes practicing an inadequate or false Islam. It offers a prescription for success—religious fervor and dedication—contrasting the impact of Hamas (the Islamic resistance organization) and Islamic Jihad (holy war) in the Gaza strip with the ineffectuality of the secular Palestine Liberation Organization. It contrasts the continuing resistance by Hezbollah (the party of God) to Israel's occupation of southern Lebanon with the passivity of Arab governments.

Iran sees a hostile United States as the prime mover behind the current peace process in the Middle East.[23] It foresees no possibility of a just or equitable outcome given the occupation of Palestinian territory by Israel and U.S. support for its client state. It opposes the negotiations, subsidizes Hezbollah and Hamas (in an amount totalling perhaps $100 million a year) and seeks to revive a rejectionist front.[24] It has attacked the agreement on Gaza and Jericho, decrying it as "unprecedented treachery" and a "stain of shame."[25]

The sincerity of Iran's leaders is not in doubt; even during the long war with Iraq they insisted that the "path to Jerusalem lies through Baghdad." Iran is especially concerned about the plight of the Shi'i in Lebanon, historically weak and poorly treated, who comprise a plurality of that country.[26] Their principal abode, the south, is now partly occupied by Israel. A traditional clerical network between Iran (Qom), Iraq (Najjaf) and south Lebanon makes the issue more immediate. Iran has opposed the disarming of Hezbollah (the Shi'i militia and, since 1992, a political party) on the grounds that it is a resistance force that must remain armed as long as Israel occupies Lebanese territory. Syria and Lebanon have accepted this argument. It suits Damascus to have Hezbollah as a source of pressure on Israel pending a settlement on the Golan. The question arises, however, of what Iran would do in the event that Syria and Israel came to an agreement on the Golan and south Lebanon, ending Hezbollah's rationale for armed resistance. (Alternatively, Israeli military pressure on Damascus to rein in Hezbollah would constrain Iran's options.)

Iran's only direct access to the Palestine issue is through southern Lebanon. Syria has allowed the stationing of some 2,000 Iranian Revolutionary Guard troops in the Beka Valley who train the Hezbollah and furnish them with regular shipments of arms from Tehran. Syria can put a limit to or end these activities at any time and will probably have to do so once an agreement with Israel is reached. Iran's rejectionist position is coming under growing pressure, and Iran will be increasingly marginalized if the Gaza-Jericho agreement is extended. Iran will then be forced to re-evaluate the level of priority that countering Israel rates in its foreign policy and the amount it is willing to pay to continue its current policies.

The Palestine question in fact subsumes several pressing issues: justice for Muslims, the fate of Shi'i, the role of Iran in Islam and Middle East politics, and United States hegemony in the region. Since 1991 Iran has taken more radical and strident positions on this last issue, organizing a rejectionist conference coinciding with the negotiations in Madrid in October and November 1991.[27] Iran has noted the exclusion of Islamist elements from the negotiations. Its stance has prompted more and more Israeli officials to depict Iran as a national security threat, citing in particular Tehran's missile programs and its quest for weapons of mass destruction. Washington has also pointed to Tehran's opposition to the peace process as an additional obstacle to the normalization of relations.

It is not clear how Iran assesses the implications of its stance in light of the PLO-Israeli developments of late 1993 and how it would deal with a peace agreement if it were deprived of Syria's support and access to Lebanon. Iran's initial rejection and subsequent acceptance of the 1989 Taif Agreement may provide a clue to Tehran's flexibility.[28] There is no pressing security stake involved in the Arab-Israeli issue for Iran as a state. However a symbolic political issue demonstrating Iran's commitment and principles has undeniable attractions. It remains doubtful whether Iran can afford to be more radical than the parties immediately affected and translate that into effective policies. Israel remains a foreign policy rather than security issue, but it could inadvertently revert from one to the other (as a result of Iran's weapons buildup or a decision by Iran to increase its indirect involvement through rejectionist groups like Hamas) stimulating an Israeli response.

NATIONAL SECURITY PRIORITIES

Iran may take positions on a broad range of issues, but its national security interests tend to be more immediate concerns. Its revolutionary rhetoric, posturing and small investments in various areas to gain influence or for nuisance-value are not one and the same as its security interests, though they are often confused. Security interests are a government's prime concerns and the areas in which a regime, feeling threatened, is prepared to rely on military power. For Iran, as for most states, these interests are concrete and proximate—centered on territorial integrity and physical security. The recent record of Iran's deployment of forces indicates what these traditional and focused interests are.

1. Two Iranian air force attacks on Iranian Mojahedin opposition bases in Iraq between April 1992 and May 1993.

2. Three air raids in Iraqi Kurdistan against Kurdish forces hostile to Tehran in the period from February 1992 to July 1993. Incursions into Iraq by Revolutionary Guard troops; Iranian statements claimed a right to "hot pursuit" insisting on their defensive motivation.[29]

3. Deployment of the elite 21st division (about 10,000 troops) to the 230-mile northern frontier opposite Azerbaijan and the commencement of military exercises (including aircraft) in August-September 1993. This activity came after Iranian warnings to Armenia in July and August against military deployments near the frontier and continued military occupation of Azerbaijan territory which had generated a flood of refugees into the frontier area near Iran.

4. Two large-scale combined arms exercises (including amphibious forces) in the Persian Gulf over the past two years. The exercises, which last several days, include the liberation of islands and harassment of a potential foe.

In all these areas Iran's security interests are clear: Iraq and opponents of the regime, vulnerability in the south and instability in the north. These are the areas in which Iran sees its primary security interests. And it is for these areas that Iran is rebuilding its military, while taking into account its experience over the past fifteen years and the lessons that it has yielded.

THE LESSONS OF
IRAN'S RECENT EXPERIENCE

The eight-year war with Iraq has been the most momentous event in the short life of the Islamic Republic. Isolated and defeated, Iran was saved from complete humiliation by Iraq's subsequent aggression against Kuwait and defeat at the hands of Western forces. These two wars provided Iran with experience directly and as an interested spectator: they gave practical instruction on the kinds of military power, their deployment and use, and about military organization and the use of force. The perspective acquired from these experiences is guiding Iran in rebuilding its military and shaping how and in what context its military will function.

The three major shortcomings of Iran's conduct of the war with Iraq were its absence of long-range planning, its failure to integrate military and manpower needs with financial and domestic resources and the poor fit between war aims and capabilities. Throughout the war, Iran instead emphasized posturing, improvisation and rhetoric for domestic consumption. Iranian leaders have alluded to some of these defects, but a critical unanswered question remains—whether the Iranian regime is able to organize itself to think in strategic military terms or to undertake long-range programs, integrating a variety of skills and organizations in pursuit of particular goals.[1]

PREPAREDNESS AND A PROFESSIONAL ARMED FORCE

In entering the war "imposed" upon it by Iraq, Iran insisted on the primary importance of morale, commitment and the necessity to mobilize a "people's war." It derided the value of modern arms and the need for training or formal organization. "The faith of the Islamic troops," said Rafsanjani repeatedly, "is stronger than Iraq's superior firepower."[2] The experience of warfare was to erase, indeed reverse, these ideas.

As the country at last emerged from the war, Iranian leaders instead embraced preparedness as an Islamic principle, implying the need for forces-in-being (a standing army).[3] Iran had earlier disparaged regular forces and subjected them to purges, leaving the country undefended and wide open to invasion. Iranian leaders attributed failure in the war to overly ambitious goals; lack of professionalism, training and equipment (reliance on a "petrol bomb mentality" in Khamenei's phrase); and poor organization and duplication.[4] The commander of the Revolutionary Guard, Mohsen Rezai, attributed Iran's poor military performance (especially in 1988) to equipment deficiencies: "They had armor and we did not...we were unarmed infantrymen against the enemy's cavalry." Rafsanjani concurred: "We were not able to equip our forces in a way which was appropriate."[5]

At the same time it was clear that the existence of two parallel military forces, the regular military and the Islamic Revolutionary Guard Corps (IRGC or Pasdaran), had complicated logistics and retarded coordination. The implication was that Iran would need to have better equipped, more integrated professional forces in the future, in part for deterrence. As Rafsanjani told the Revolutionary Guard:

> We are duty bound to reorganize ourselves in such a way that we will not face a similar attack. We have gradually come to realize...that topics such as rank, hierarchy, salary—a just order of pay—and the like, constitute the necessities for an armed force. However if we are to count on the IRGC as an armed force, if the regime is to survive to serve God, it must not think that when it is attacked it can fight with Molotov cocktails. Such an armed force must be so prepared that others will not dare attack it.[6]

Deficiencies in training, coordination and logistics were all too apparent. In naval matters, the war showed the vulnerability of Iran's maritime assets—without air cover or sound intelligence and communications, with sensors and radar that were barely operational after 1987. These weaknesses underlined the need for spare parts, maintenance and resupply or for substitute weapons systems that could be domestically serviced or replaced. This raised the question of future supply, since the air force's and most of the navy's equipment, the areas most in need of attention, had been purchased from the United States by the Shah.

SELF-RELIANCE AND DIVERSIFICATION OF ARMS SUPPLIERS
The war also underscored the vulnerability of arms importing nations to supplier interruptions or embargoes. Especially after 1986 when Operation Staunch was more rigorously implemented by the United States, cutting off Iranian access to spare parts and new arms, Iran had difficulty sustaining its war effort. As the war dragged on, cannibalizing parts and improvising repairs and maintenance became harder, replacements scarcer and more costly. As a result, in postwar Iran, "self-reliance" has become the watchword, meaning in practice a mixture of domestic production, diversification of sources of supply and stockpiling of arms and spare parts sufficient to carry on in the event of major supply interruptions.[7] The problems of equipment originating from a variety of sources, especially when it entails different weapons systems (aircraft from the United States and Russia in inventory at the same time, for instance) need not be belabored here. Suffice

it to say that Iran's experience during the war proved the hazards of juggling differing parallel logistical requirements. During its war with Iraq, Iran had to find arms wherever they were available; by the end of the war it had supplies from more than twenty sources, and in the process it shifted to a considerable extent to Eastern bloc arms. Its experience with fluctuating supply sources and materiel and the exigencies of switching types of arms in midstream gave Iran a powerful incentive in future arms agreements to emphasize "the transfer of technology for the manufacturing of defensive arms."[8]

To seek self-reliance to reduce vulnerability to supply cut-offs makes sense, but whether it is practicable is another matter. Adaptation, reverse engineering and improvisation may be possible where absolutely necessary, creating rudimentary skills and industries, but these do not equal an arms industry. Iran now puts heightened emphasis on repairs, technical training and arms production. It produces "over 49 types of ammunition," trains its own pilots, repairs most of its own aircraft, designs and produces local missiles (battlefield variety) and copies (through reverse engineering) missiles like the Tow and Stinger, produces a type of tank, and can extend the range of aircraft by adding external fuel tanks. It is also developing a light passenger/trainer plane, the Swallow (Parastu), with the aim of eventually producing a fighter/bomber. Defense industries have been reorganized and centralized since the war, in hopes that past experience will inform future projects.[9]

In theory domestic arms industries can save money, local costs being less than those of suppliers. According to one source, 80 percent of the missiles used by Iran were of domestic manufacture. Iran's savings from its arms industries have been estimated as between $900 million and $2 billion per year.[10] Despite this capacity Iran does not claim that local industry can replace imports; self-reliance is relative and is to be achieved in the production, in the words of the defense minister for logistics, of standard equipment, which "we use a lot."[11] There are obvious problems with defense industries that attempt to go beyond repair work to supplant imports. They tend to be too expensive—unit costs being high and the prospects for exports being low—and they can rarely match qualitatively the equipment that can be imported. This is especially true in the Persian Gulf where Iran has to consider that its adversaries will have access to highly advanced U.S. equipment. Alternatively, if local defense production is intended for repair, maintenance, ammunition and simpler equipment, then it can hardly be considered a solution to the problem of supply where major equipment is concerned (aircraft, for instance).

Iran's insistence on this approach may be more rhetorical than real, intended instead for political purposes—to appeal to national pride and to reassure. As the object of an arms embargo Iran gained considerable practical (and costly) experience in the clandestine "gray" market for arms: in establishing networks of purchasing agents, creating cutouts and front companies, doctoring end-use papers, in bribery, transhipments and the art of false documentation. These tactics enabled it to prolong the war. Moreover, Iran derived a political lesson from this experience, on which it may be building for its nuclear, biological and chemical programs. Briefly put, embargoes can be circumvented and allies can be divided; hence Khamenei's statement: "If we intend to obtain the goods we need from anywhere we wish, we have the power to do so."[12] Stated otherwise, given sufficient cunning and resources, anything is possible.

THE TECHNOLOGY EDGE AND THE COMPLACENCY OF INTERNATIONAL BODIES

Iran had a ringside seat for Desert Storm, enabling it to closely consider the military implications of that conflict. On a general level the most impressive aspect was the yawning gap between the military performance of an advanced state and that of a heavily armed (but inept) developing country. It would be difficult for Iran, which considers the United States as capable of repeating a Desert Storm, to escape the conclusion that this gap in conventional weapons and warfare is unlikely to be bridged anytime soon. If anything was underscored by the impressive logistical feats of the war, it was the centrality of air power and intelligence, the emphasis on maneuver and the limited casualties sustained. Nothing could contrast more starkly with Iran's repeated and ultimately ineffectual offensives over a period of ninety-five months.[13]

In general, both wars reinforced the sense of paranoia and embattlement in Iran; the Iran-Iraq war was depicted as part of the U.S.-led conspiracy to suppress the revolution; Desert Storm is seen as an example of the excesses of U.S. power when unconstrained by other states. In the first war, Iran saw the United Nations remain silent when it was invaded by Iraq, yet the U.N. accommodated the United States when it chose to react to the Kuwait invasion. Iran's sense of grievance at this unequal treatment was barely assuaged by the secretary-general's eventual formal designation of Iraq as the aggressor in the Iran-Iraq War in autumn 1991. Both wars reinforced Iran's determination to rebuild its military forces, increase its self-reliance and place little faith in international institutions in security matters. But before turning to the policies it has adopted as a result, it is important to assess the most critical areas in which the recent wars have left their mark on Iranian perspectives and policies.

MISSILES AND CHEMICAL WEAPONS: BITTER EXPERIENCE; APPROPRIATE LESSONS?

The most traumatic chapter for Iran in the war with Iraq was the use of chemical weapons and missiles. In both areas Iran came off the worse, nurturing a sense of grievance and a determination to prevent a repetition in the future. As a participant (or in Iran's view, victim) this harrowing experience has conditioned how it regards these weapons.

Missile Use in the Two Wars
By 1984 Iraq had virtual control of the air, which it used sporadically to bomb Tehran. Iran responded by firing short-range missiles from just inside Iran, taking advantage of Baghdad's proximity to the border. The pace of these exchanges increased as Baghdad stepped up its attacks following Iran's ground offensives. In the spring of 1988 an intensive series of exchanges known as the "war of the cities" saw Iraq launch 190 Scud missiles against Iran's 70 to 75. Whereas Iraq was able to fire these in salvos (seven on February 29, 1988) Iran was able to fire only one missile per day. Iraq's missile advantages came in addition to its air superiority (its air force was roughly seven times larger than Iran's). Its missiles, especially after the development of the Al-Husayn in 1987, were more accurate, plentiful and had longer ranges than Iran's. Iraqi stocks appeared limitless while Iran, scouring the world market in desperation, was unable to secure adequate numbers.[14] This advantage put Iraq in a position of control over the escalation of the missile and air wars.

Iran allegedly suffered 3,000 fatalities from air and missile attacks in 1987. Tehran claimed that of its total losses (133,000 lives) some 11,000 were civilian deaths.[15] Even so this number understates the political effects of Iraqi attacks. By taking the war to Iran, Iraq terrorized the civilian population, which began to clamor for shelters and to desert the cities in large numbers. Iraq thus imposed a political cost on Iran's leadership for continuing the conflict. The Iranian government's conduct of the war became politically damaging, especially as it was unable to offer the population any defense or to riposte in kind. These direct assaults on civilian morale had appreciable effects which would have been all the greater had the Iraqi aircraft or missiles carried chemical warheads. As Iraq had shown little restraint in using chemical weapons on the battlefield, Iranian leaders probably felt it unlikely that Iraq would hold off from using them against civilians. The perception that Iran was at the mercy of an Iraq commanding vast weapons stocks, unconstrained internationally and with little or no compunction as to humanitarian values or morality was surely unnerving to citizenry and government alike. We cannot be certain whether the missile attacks (and the implicit threat of chemical payloads) played a key role in Iran's decision to sue for peace. It is significant, however, that in victory Iraq attributed a key role to missiles. In describing the background to Iran's decision, one Iraqi source reported that Iran's political and military leaders had unanimously agreed that "the course of the war had changed in favor of Iraq since the onset of the missile war." Moreover, an Iraqi analyst claimed that in future conflicts Iraqi strategy would be based on the early, surprise and intensive use of missiles.[16] It is unlikely that Iranian defense planners have missed this probable strategy of their closest enemy, nor that they have neglected to act on its implications.

Desert Storm underscored other points. First, unlike aircraft bombing, missile penetration was not so dependent on the skills of a pilot and the range was much greater. Second, the terrorizing effect Iraqi missile attacks had on Israel was out of all proportion to any possible military utility.[17] Third, even the odd, chance missile hit could amplify this terror. Fourth, mobile missiles were survivable, effective if well deployed and difficult to locate.

Observations about Missile Use

What lessons has Iran derived about missiles from these wars and applied to its own procurement policies? First is the need for a retaliatory capability. Rafsanjani has specifically described this as the only way to deter Saddam Hussein from attacks on towns.[18] He also implied that while Iran preferred to avoid using missiles, it would have to retain them to threaten retaliation and hence as a deterrent.[19] This outlook emerged from the war with Iraq and was reinforced by Iraq's continued missile buildup during 1988-90 and the revelations in 1990-91 about the advances it had made (in cooperation with other states). From this perspective, Iran's incentive to acquire missiles has not been diminished; Iraq may well prove to be but a temporarily dormant threat. At the same time Iran has drawn conclusions about the war:

We learned a great deal in the course of the war...many techniques, we gained experience in weaponry and we learned what weapons have what effects nowadays... [We acquired] the technical capability... to produce the most important and essential weapons today — *missiles are the most important weapons today* and we have solved the most important problems regarding the missile industries, and now what concerns us is what to produce, how many to produce...[20]

Rafsanjani assured Iranians after the cease-fire that Iran now had a device that, in the event of another war, would guard against any replay of the war of the cities.[21] During Desert Storm Iranian commentators, with this experience still fresh in mind, cited the importance of missiles for the "big lesson" they taught, hence Iran's need for them "to boost the defense capabilities of the country and minimize possible enemy air and missile strikes against economic centers as well as military forces."[22]

Iran was incensed at the USSR for putting "an unbelievable and unacceptable quantity of missiles" into the hands of a "lunatic country."[23] Its own desperate and unsuccessful scramble for missiles in 1987-88 and the ability of the suppliers to use their deliveries for leverage compelled Iran to shift to East bloc arms sources, principally the People's Republic of China and North Korea. At the same time the embargo forced Iran to rely more on its own resources and to develop them. It launched a crash program for building missiles.

It developed battlefield missiles including the Oghab (eagle) and Shahin (falcon); in April 1989 it announced the manufacture of a new missile with a range of 200 kilometers (120 miles).[24] In January 1991 Iran announced that it had started mass production of long-range missiles. Desert Storm reinforced the perceived need for missiles while the history of supply problems dictated the accelerated development of the domestic production base in tandem with increased stockpiling for future emergencies, preferably from a wide range of suppliers.

Although missiles may be necessary as a deterrent, there is room for debate as to whether they are cost-effective or decisive. In early 1993 Iran's defense minister argued that at $2.5 million per (Scud-B) missile, they were neither.[25] On the other hand local production might reduce costs. Missiles may well be the weapon of choice for states without dependable access to advanced aircraft or adequate manpower and technical skills to make full use of a modern air force. A missile force may appeal to states that politically distrust their professional militaries. Missiles may seem to be a shortcut because they separate a state's capacity to punish an enemy from its ability to achieve results on the battlefield, allowing it to "extract enormous costs from an adversary's population despite the manifest poor performance of [its] own military in combat."[26] The idea of missiles as a shortcut or substitute for a modern air force is more attractive to a nonspecialist than to an expert, however.

Lessons about Chemical Weaponry

Missiles' military appeal as a deterrent, their political appeal as weapons that cast a long shadow regionally and their implicit decoupling of destructive ability from military expertise make them indispensable to a country such as Iran that has been on the receiving end of salvos and that fears a recurrence. Iran has drawn similar conclusions from its war experiences which inform its current military programs regarding chemical weapons.

Iran's experience of chemical weapons parallels its history with missiles. Iran found itself at a loss technologically, betrayed by international silence and once again unable to acquire the means to deter Iraq's continued use of these weapons. The possibility that Iraq might combine both chemical arms and missiles would certainly have occurred to Iranian defense officials.

Iraq's use of chemical weapons was effective as much for its initial surprise and lasting intimidation as for its operational utility. Rather specific conditions of warfare favored its effective use: Iran's massed offensives, the intense heat, inadequate protection and poor discipline made its soldiers vulnerable. Between 1983 and 1988 Iraq also improved its ability to use this weaponry on the battlefield.[27] Iraq graduated from using chemical weapons as a last-resort defense in the earlier periods to making them part of tactical offensives to reclaim Iraqi territory, especially against Fao and Shalamcheh in spring 1988. By this time they were especially effective operationally.

One of the factors that traditionally militated against the use of chemical weapons was the international opprobrium brought to bear against any country even known to possess them. Iraq might have been more reluctant to resort to their continued use—which had become almost routine after six years—if it had had to pay heavily for doing so. In practice international criticism was limited. The rest of the world seemed to perceive some moral equivalence between a state gassing its neighbor and the neighbor launching repeated futile, "human wave" attacks of teenagers over minefields. Even after the war, at the Paris conference on chemical weapons in 1989, the United States and its allies were unwilling to condemn Iraq's use of chemical weapons in forthright terms. Various U.N. investigations had documented this use and individual states had offered humanitarian assistance, but the United States was reluctant to endanger Iraq's war effort by accusing it.

Iran's use of chemical arms is disputed. If it used them it did so on a small scale and infrequently. Many official statements claimed that it possessed some capability but did not exercise it on moral grounds. Iran threatened to resort to preventive measures in self-defense, however, if Iraq continued its chemical attacks.[28] Some observers have suggested that Iran's use was limited as much by capability as by ethical concerns.[29] Whatever the reason, the results are clear: if Iran used chemical arms it did so on only one or two occasions, both times on a small scale with limited results; Iraq became more confident with time and expanded their use quite effectively, unconstrained by international outcry or moral concerns. Iran was unable to develop the means to counteract their effects or to deter their use. In short, during the course of the war Iran was unable to acquire a retaliatory capability. It lacked this weapon in its inventory, and as was the case with missiles, it was unable to acquire adequate stocks because of the arms embargo.

Iran claimed it suffered 5,000 fatalities from chemical attacks and nine times that number wounded, while never resorting to these weapons itself, "even as a means of retaliation."[30] Iran has never stated that these weapons, any more than missiles, were decisive in the war, though it has often alluded to their open and flagrant misuse, condoned by the West's silence, as sign of a conspiracy (and of a double standard) where Islamic Iran is concerned.[31] The sense that Iran was fighting not just Iraq but the world—with unequal weapons—added to the demoralizing effect of Iraq's preponderance in missiles and chemical weapons.[32]

Desert Storm would have tended to confirm the Iranian perception that a retaliatory capacity constituting a deterrent is the best defense in this area. Despite operational questions (given the coalition's use of surprise and maneuver) and command and control problems that would have reduced the effectiveness of chemical weapons, the fact remains that Iraq did not use its extensive chemical arms stocks against the allies. A very plausible inference is that Baghdad was deterred by the threat of a riposte in kind, of escalation to the nuclear level or simply of a major conventional response (such as a widening of war aims, decapitation). In short, Iraq was deterred by the threat of unacceptable retaliation.

IRAN'S LEADERS AND THEIR CONCLUSIONS FROM THE WAR

The experience of Iran's leaders during the course of the war has dominated the way they have looked at security since. The first, overwhelmingly clear political lesson was that Iran could not rely on the international community where its defense was concerned, that some states would not be bound by rules governing the conduct of war, and that Iran should seek preparedness accordingly.[33] Rafsanjani made this point clearly and broadly in two speeches in late 1988: "The main problems of chemical industries both defensive and offensive, have been solved completely by our experts...." Iran, as result of its recent experience, "should completely equip [itself] both in the offensive and defensive use of chemical, bacteriological and radiological weapons" (in Persian: *shin, mim, rey).* "From now on you should make use of this opportunity and perform this task."[34]

Iranian leaders acknowledged that they had worked on the research and development of chemical and biological weapons. In reference to Iran's indigenous arms industry, the commander of the Revolutionary Guard, Mohsen Rezai, noted that among the thirteen industrial groups in research and production there were "rocket, chemical, bacteriological and nuclear industries *[shimayayi-microbi-hasteh'i].*"[35] Rafsanjani observed in 1988, "The production of chemical weapons and laying one's hands on chemical materials is not a difficult job for a country like Iran. With its great pharmaceutical factories and very high level chemical experts, Iran would not find it difficult to do this. [Iran] has the power to manufacture all sorts of chemical materials which are customary in the armies of the world...[it] has the power of mass production."[36]

During the war Iran's leaders came to see that claiming to have the capability without using it gained little: it did not deter Iraq's use and it elicited neither sympathy nor a response from the West. Thus Iran's leaders arrived at the conclusion that preparing against a future technological surprise had another side: as with missiles, effective deterrence required a retaliatory capability. Desert Storm confirmed what history had demonstrated since World War I (see Table 1). Chemical arms are only used when an adversary is unable to respond.[37] Within a few months of the cease-fire with Iraq, Iran's leaders were looking ahead. Rafsanjani asserted in October 1988, "Chemical and biological weapons are [the] poor man's atomic bombs and can easily be produced. We should at least consider them for our defence."[38]

Besides the imperative of self-reliance and the need for a deterrent against outlaw states like Iraq, Iran's leaders see their interest in these weapons as justified by the unreliability of the U.N. Security Council. Iran's representatives to the United Nations repeatedly warned of the "dangerous precedent for the further use of these deadly weapons" set by inaction. They have also stressed the need for joint efforts "to put a stop to such a calamity which poses a serious threat in future."[39]

AN APPROACH TO SECURITY CONDITIONED BY WAR

Iran's attitudes to military power and security are comprehensible seen in light of the formative, desperate years of the Iran-Iraq War. In this per-

Table 1   DOCUMENTED EPISODES OF POISON GAS WARFARE SINCE WORLD WAR ONE

Date	User	Chemical Agent	Delivery Means
1919	British forces intervening in the Russian Civil War	Mustard gas	Artillery
1925	Spanish forces in Morocco	Mustard gas	Aircraft bombing
1934	Soviet forces intervening against Muslim insurgents in Xinjiang, Central Asia	Mustard gas	Aircraft bombing
1935-40	Italian Forces in Ethiopia	Mustard gas	Aircraft spraying and bombing
1937-45	Japanese forces in China	Mustard gas and lewisite	Aircraft bombing
1966-67	Egyptian forces intervening in the [North] Yemeni Civil War	Phosgene and mustard gas	Aircraft bombing
1983-88	Iraqi forces in the Gulf War	Mustard and tabun	Aircraft bombing

Source: Sussex/Harvard Information Bank on Chemical and Biological Weapons Armament and Arms Limitation.

spective, the "imposed war" and the scant U.N. or Western reaction to Iraqi aggression were parts of a conspiracy to strangle revolutionary Iran. The West condoned Iraq's use of chemical weapons and the East sold it missiles; both supplied arms to Baghdad while denying Iran access to arms. Subsequently a cease-fire was engineered by an international entity, leaving Iraq in possession of Iranian territory.

Militarily, the lessons for Iran were clear enough: to avoid technological surprises a country must develop a wide range of arms; without a retaliatory capability, deterrence is unworkable; reliance on the United Nations, treaties and the like is no substitute for self-reliance; problems with suppliers can be avoided through domestic arms production; access to technology can be had by diversifying supply sources and seeking transfer rights; improving the quality of conventional arms requires additional training of and discipline among the forces that are equipped with them. Desert Storm demonstrated the inherent difficulties in trying to match the advanced nations in conventional weaponry. These are compounded by costs, difficulty of assimilation and unavailability. Preparedness requires a strong military; in the short term it can be achieved by acquiring missiles and through research, development and possibly deployment of weapons of mass destruction.

ARMS POLICIES AND PROGRAMS

Iran's arms policies are guided not only by the lessons of recent wars but also by the objective conditions of its armed forces, budget constraints, the availability of arms and its own aspirations internationally. Iran is now acting on the lessons derived from its experience and understanding of war in the rebuilding its military forces. Some 50 percent of its inventory was destroyed in the war; the remainder has been rendered largely obsolescent by inadequate servicing, lack of parts and the passage of time. As it rebuilds Iran is modernizing, seeking the most advanced weapons systems on the market where possible. This is not unusual and not in itself an indicator of aggressive intent. By most criteria—its weapons inventory in 1979 or its smaller neighbors' arms programs, for instance—Iran's conventional military buildup is still reasonable in scale. It is based on immediate needs as well as the lessons of war.

Iran's military effort also demonstrates a determination to play a major international role. Modernizing its armed forces could advance this objective. However, translating arms into military effectiveness depends on a number of things—force structure, doctrine, force levels and training of manpower, supplies and so forth. By these criteria, Iran has far to go before it becomes a significant military power in terms of conventional means.

BLOC OBSOLESCENCE

Indeed it has some way to go before it attains its 1979 capability. Iran emerged from the war with Iraq as a shadow of what it had been a decade earlier. Iran lost so much equipment, one expert reflected, that it had to choose "between a crippling investment in conventional arms—which it has costed at something approaching $25 billion—and accepting long-term inferiority with Iraq." From this standpoint "Iran could scarcely be expected to accept the force levels it had at the end of the Iran-Iraq war."[1] Moreover, the equipment resulting from a decade of buying whatever was available was a logistical nightmare—nine types of tanks, seven types of antitank missiles, and a motley assortment of weapons systems of varying sophistication, generation and provenance—enormously complicating maintenance and support.[2]

Iran's military reconstruction is not simply a question of replacement or rebuilding, restocking and modernization, which are a matter of resources. Faced with overall obsolescence, Iran has to upgrade virtually all of its major weapons systems, especially aircraft, air defense and armor. Besides standardization, however, a clearer idea of force structure and priorities along with a more sharply defined military doctrine are necessary as well.

Hence the end to the war with Iraq brought no peace dividend. Iran was proud that it emerged from the war with few debts and that it had limited military spending.[3] But as Rafsanjani noted, peacetime defense expenditures would have to be higher because of salaries, reconstruction, replacement and restocking.[4]

FORCE STRUCTURE

The decision to move toward better trained-forces and advanced arms marked a retreat from the ideologically motivated "scorched-earth" tactics and people's armies promulgated before actual experience of war. This shift implies a recruitment policy favoring skills and education over political loyalty. Historically, the regime has distrusted the regular military. It organized the Islamic Republic Guards Corps (IRGC—also known as the Pasdaran or Sepah) to offset the military. Subsequently the Basij (Sepah-e Basij), a popular militia with minimal training but avowed commitment to the regime, was formed under the command of the IRGC.[5] However the war with Iraq necessitated the reconstitution and expansion of the regular forces. Their role in the war rehabilitated them in terms of reputation although they are still the object of distrust.

The tensions between the ideologically committed forces preferred by the regime and the skilled career cadre forces required for national (as opposed to regime) security have not been resolved in any operational doctrine. In practice the two forces coexist to check one another (see Table 2). As long as Iran perceives no urgent external threat, it can afford to pamper the Pasdaran. Considered the guardians of the revolution, they are assigned a cultural mission consisting of generating political support for the regime, monitoring opponents, recruiting loyal supporters of the regime and tending the message of the revolution. At times they give support to oppressed peoples (for instance, Hezbollah) or worthy governments (such as the Sudanese).

The Pasdaran trains the much larger Basij forces, which constitute reserves to be mobilized in crises. Training includes a degree of political-religious indoctrination. With a large manpower base to draw on for reserves, the Pasdaran serves as the nucleus of future revolutionary forces—politically reliable, however rudimentary their military skills. In addition, both Basij and Pasdaran are being used in domestic reconstruction projects, somewhat lightening the burden of military expenditures on civil society.

The Pasdaran and regular military have been slated for integration since 1988 in order to combine commitment and professionalism and to

Table 2   COMPARATIVE STRENGTHS OF IRAN'S PROFESSIONAL ARMED FORCES AND REVOLUTIONARY GUARD

	Professional Armed Forces	Revolutionary Guard
Total Forces	353,000	120,000
Army	320,000	100,000
Navy	18,000	20,000
Air Force	15,000	0

Source: *The Military Balance 1993-94.*

permit a more coherent doctrine and organizational structure to emerge. Their missions have been defined: the Pasdaran for internal security ("defending the revolution") and the regular military for defense against external threats.[6] The 1984 decision to develop an air force for the Pasdaran has been scrapped, but of its 150,000 members, some 20,000 are naval forces, possibly with three brigades of marines.

The Pasdaran appears to have first choice among certain arms, including missiles, fast patrol boats and the new Kilo-class submarines. In terms of Iran's politics the Pasdaran should be seen as an important interest group as opposed to a virtually autonomous institution within Iran's power structure.[7] It carries on its own distinct military-diplomatic relationships with other states, favoring Syria, North Korea, China and Pakistan, and presumably acts quasi-autonomously in the choice of arms purchased.

Because Pasdaran troops have limited skills and education, they are unsuitable recipients of advanced weapons that require elaborate maintenance and training or complex logistical maneuvering. Iran's emphasis on missiles, which are under the Pasdaran's operational control, may be an attempt to capitalize on its loyalty without stretching its practical capabilities (as the elaborate infrastructure necessary for an advanced air force would).

The professional cadre of the regular military consists of some 50,000 men and the balance (approximately 250,000) is made up of two-year conscripts. The professional core's relatively small size reduces the costs of keeping standing forces and limits its political weight. In the absence of a compelling threat the pressure to expand this component will be slight. Given time Iran hopes to be able to reconcile professionalism and ideological commitment to the regime and build a modern fighting force totally committed to the revolution. It is not clear that this is feasible, however; the technical proficiency, organizational loyalty and professional pride that is needed to attract educated and skilled manpower is not compatible with the kinds of rewards, perks and autonomy enjoyed by the less proficient parallel forces of the Pasdaran. Without greater respect, rewards and professional autonomy, it is unlikely that the regular military can be developed as the skilled force capable of using advanced arms effectively that some planners acknowledge a need for.

As a powerful institution with a vested interest in the status quo, the Pasdaran is unlikely to endorse or facilitate a shift of resources to a more professional force. Its attitude will certainly complicate a major revision of doctrine or redistribution of resources.

Can the regime trust the regular military enough to encourage recruitment based on technical competence (or potential competence) so that a military that functions as a modern fighting force can emerge? Or will it continue to favor the Pasdaran as more reliable, despite the negative implications for the goal of building a modern military? The answers to these questions are by no means self-evident, hence Iran's efforts to benefit from the lessons of its wartime experience and to rebuild its force structure and equipment will be neither smooth nor rapid. Questions will linger about the effective integration of the Pasdaran with the regular military and the creation of a unified command structure.[8]

DOMESTIC PRODUCTION AND PATTERNS OF PROCUREMENT

Domestic production of conventional arms has been limited to ammunition, spare parts and the simpler systems that Iran used most often during the war. Iran expanded wartime production out of necessity, and afterward it continued based on the assumption that local production reduced costs and provided a buffer against supply cutoffs. Yet local production costs often exceed those of imported systems unless the unit cost of equipment can be spread out, preferably by sales abroad. Yet exporting is not always possible because of stiff competition for shares of foreign markets. Furthermore, exclusive reliance on domestic production may bring about a drastic reduction in the quality of weapons systems. Since its southern neighbors in the Gulf have access to advanced systems, Iran would be severely handicapping itself if it chose this course.

The origins of Iran's arms shifted radically during the war. Purchases from China, North Korea, the European states and a diverse group of nations replaced a stockpile that had been largely U.S. supplied. Between 1985 and 1988, China accounted for 34 percent and the European states another 41 percent. During the period 1989-92, Russia and China accounted for the vast bulk (64 percent and 16 percent respectively) while Europe's share declined to 8 percent.[9] The pattern of supply from Eastern bloc sources reflects an intention to replace the remaining arms in inventory with new arms. In the case of aircraft parts and other major systems, these will have to come from Russia. From Iran's perspective Russia's need for foreign exchange and its relatively efficient arms industries, manage to insulate the arms relationship from the volatility typical when political considerations are uppermost. Two caveats apply to this, however. First, Russia's ability to provide the full integrated follow-on services required of a major supplier is somewhat doubtful. Second, while Russia may have an interest in arms sales generally, this does not dictate sales of specific systems. Consequently it may be susceptible to U.S. pressure to forego or reverse sales of specific weapons systems objectionable to the West. From the U.S. perspective the shift in suppliers is worrisome because it reduces its leverage. North Korea and China have been reluctant to curb sales, especially of missiles. They have not been willing to abide by strict regulations and they have been less than candid with the United States about their actual deliveries.[10] China and North Korea's arms sales to such states as Syria and Pakistan, which may be cooperating with Iran militarily, compounds the problem for the United States. If intensified, such cooperation among these and other quasi-pariah states could coalesce into an alliance (possibly with Iraq). Although an alliance of "rogue" states marginalized by world affairs would be founded on weakness, it would still have the capacity to cause considerable nuisance.

For the time being, Iran has access to advanced arms as long as Moscow is willing to supply them and Tehran can pay. It is not clear that either condition will persist. Moscow may come under pressure from the United States, or take exception to Iran's policies, and Iran may find it hard to spare the foreign exchange required for a multiyear program. Even if the relationship continues there is no guarantee that Russia can provide the after-sales service support base essential for the systems it supplies, notably aircraft. Above all the impact of the transfer of Russian aircraft can do little to enhance Iran's capabilities in the short to medium term. Switching suppliers and systems requires a transition period of at least a decade judging from Egypt's experience since 1977. In Iran's case it may be longer if only because of its determination to keep its remaining U.S.-supplied aircraft in service, which will complicate logistics and training.

MILITARY EFFORT IN PERSPECTIVE

In comparison with its earlier military efforts and with those of its neighbors, and bearing in mind losses from the war and the supply cutoff caused by poor relations with the United States, Iran's current buildup is not excessive. It is worth emphasizing, however, that in an era of diminished resources the burden of military expenditures is greater, and their opportunity costs higher. Thus a sustained allocation of resources to this sector would signal a determination to attain military power at a high cost, reflecting the high value attached to military power.

Iran embarked on a significant arms import program after 1989-90. The first five-year economic plan (1989-93) allocated $2 billion of foreign exchange per year to finance this. Between 1989 and 1992 Iran ordered $6.7 billion worth of equipment. Deliveries worth $1.5 billion were made in 1991. Iran concluded arms agreements totalling $17.5 billion between 1985 and 1992, making it the third largest importer of arms in the Third World.[11] The pace of Iran's buildup accelerated, especially between 1989 and 1991. However, both in terms of the effort and inventories of its neighbors and in relation to Iran's own inventory in 1979 (a reasonable baseline before the Iran-Iraq War) Iran's current arms imports are not in themselves extravagant (as Tables 3 and 4 show).

Iran's military arsenal, even when anticipated deliveries are counted, remains smaller than it was at the beginning of the revolution. By all indices—combat aircraft, main battle tanks, major artillery pieces, attack helicopters—Iran's arsenal is one-half to one-third its prewar size. Military manpower has grown from about 240,000 to 528,000 reflecting mobilization in war and growth in population from 38 million to 58 million.[12]

The decline in Iran's relative military position is most striking vis-à-vis its neighbors, Iraq and Saudi Arabia, which have shorter coastlines on the Gulf and populations of between one-third and one-quarter the size of Iran's. Between 1979 and 1991 Iran's tank force dropped from 1,700 to 700, operational aircraft from 445 to a maximum of 150, helicopters from 600 to less than 200. Saudi Arabia followed an opposite pattern: its combat aircraft doubled to 253 and its tanks to 700; its armored brigades doubled; its mechanized infantry quadrupled; and its artillery battalions expanded from three to five.[13] Despite Iran's engagement in an eight-year war that consumed equipment and resources, it has consistently spent much less on defense and imported far fewer arms than Saudi Arabia; for example Iran's arms imports for the period 1986-92 totalled $17.5 billion—less than one-third of Saudi Arabia's ($63.6 billion), which was at peace.[14]

Iraq is a similar story. In 1979 Iraq was far weaker than its neighbor in terms of numbers and quality of weapons systems, with less than one-third of Iran's level of strength in aircraft and helicopters. Iran's air force manpower was double that of Iraq and its naval manpower quadruple. Iran's arms imports between 1975 and 1980 had been nearly double Iraq's—$15 billion versus $8 billion.[15] During the 1980s, with access to arms and funds, Iraq reversed this imbalance. By 1986 Iraq enjoyed superiority in all areas: it outnumbered Iran by a 7:1 ratio in aircraft (500 versus 70); a 4.5:1 ratio in tanks (4,500 to 1,000) and boasted similar advantages across the board.[16] Arms transfers reiterate the pattern. Between 1984 and 1991 Iraq received twice the value of arms as Iran ($34.9 billion versus $16.1 billion).[17]

The skewed capabilities of Iran and its smaller neighbor continued after the cease-fire of 1988. Iran's military effort slackened and its defense

Table 3   ARMS LEVELS IN IRAN, IRAQ AND SAUDI ARABIA, SELECTED YEARS

Year	Country	Combat Aircraft	Tanks	Naval Vessels	Artillery	Military Expenditures
1979	Iran (under the Shah)	447	1,985	14	710	$9.94 billion *(1978-79)*
	Iraq	339	1,900	12	800	$2.02 *(1978)*
	Saudi Arabia	178	350	0	n.a.	$14.18 *(1979-80)*
1986	Iran (during war)	70[a]	1,000	13-15	600+	$14.09 billion *(1985-86)*
	Iraq (during war)	500	4,500	12	5,500	$12.87[a] *(1985)*
	Saudi Arabia	216	450	13	505[a]	$17.69[b] *(1985-86)*
1989	Iran (at war's end)	70 (121)	500	18	800	$5.77 billion[b] *(1989-90)*
	Iraq (at war's end)	513	5,500	13	500[a](sp)[c] 3,000 (t)[d]	$12.87[a] *(1988)*
	Saudi Arabia	179	550	17	275 (sp) 168[a](t)	$14.69[b] *(1989)*
1991	Iran	262 (+112)	700+	18	1,300 + (t, sp)	$4.27 billion[a,] *(1991)*
	Iraq	316[a]	2,300[a]	1[a]	1,200[a](t)	$8.61[b] *(1990)*
	Saudi Arabia	293	700	17	160 (sp) 90 (+140)(t)	$35.51[a] *(1991)*

n.a.=not available   a. Estimated value   c. sp=self-propelled artillery
                          b. Defense budget   d. t=towed artillery

Sources: All 1979 figures are from *The Military Balance, 1979-80;* naval vessels include destroyers, submarines, frigates an missile craft; artillery category was called "guns and howitzers"; Iraq had "about" 339 combat aircraft. All 1986 figures a from *The Military Balance, 1986-87;* naval vessels include destroyers, frigates and missile craft; Iran had "perhaps" 1,000 tanks and "some" 600+ artillery; up to two Iranian ships were nonoperational; Iraq had "some" 500 combat aircraft and 4,500 tanks. All 1989 figures are from *The Military Balance, 1989-90;* of Iran's 121 combat aircraft, only 70 were serviceab tanks are main battle tanks only; Iran had "perhaps" 500 main battle tanks and 800 artillery pieces; Iraq had "some" 513 combat aircraft, 5,500 main battle tanks and 3,000 towed artillery. All 1991 figures are from *The Military Balance, 1992-93* naval vessels includes destroyers, submarines, frigates and missile craft; tanks are main battle tanks only; Iran's 1991 com aircraft include 112 acquired from Iraq during the Gulf War (most are probably nonoperational); less than 50 percent of Iran's U.S. aircraft are serviceable; the number of Iraq's self-propelled artillery is unknown; Saudi Arabia has 140 towed a tillery in storage; Saudi military expenditures include contributions to Gulf War allies and arms purchases during the war

Table 4   THE IRANIAN ARMED FORCES, 1978-79 AND 1993-94

Iranian Forces	1978-79	1993-94
Defense Spending	$9.94 billion[a]	$1.2 billion[b]
Total Armed Forces	413,000	473,000
Army	285,000	320,000
IRGC[c]	—	100,000
Navy	28,000	18,000
IRGC	—	20,000
Air Force	100,000	15,000
Combat Aircraft	459	293[d] (+112)[e]
Main Battle Tanks	760	700+
Helicopters	785	356
Artillery	710[f]	2,300

a. $9.94 billion was Iran's 1978-79 defense expenditure of 700 billion rials according to national (Iranian) definitions.
b. Iran's official defense budget figure for 1993, not including arms purchases, is 368 billion rials ($1.2 billion).
c. IRGC, the Iranian Revolutionary Guard Corps, did not exist before the Iranian revolution.
d. Of Iran's 1993-94 combat aircraft, "probably" less than 50 percent of U.S. aircraft are serviceable (at least 100 aircraft not serviceable).
e. The 112 additional aircraft were flown from Iraq to Iran during the Gulf War. They are probably nonoperational and are not included in the 293.
f. 1978-79 artillery figures are for guns and howitzers.

Sources: *The Military Balance, 1978-79*, and *The Military Balance, 1993-94*.

expenditures dropped precipitously—some 60 percent before stabilizing: from $9.9 billion in 1988 to $5.7 billion in 1989 to $3.18 billion in 1990, to $3.77 billion in 1991. Iraq's expenditures declined less steeply despite much larger stocks. Iraq had doubled its combat aircraft, helicopters and tanks and tripled its artillery pieces. It had a sevenfold advantage over Iran in aircraft and fifteenfold advantage in tanks (see Table 3).[18]

Even after Desert Storm Iraq retained its superiority over Iran in key areas. An official U.S. assessment pointed to Iraq's formidable fighting force compared with its neighbors: with three times the number of armored vehicles as Iran (2,000 tanks, 3,000 armored personnel carriers), 1,000 artillery pieces and possibly several hundred missiles and some Scud launchers. Another report put Iraq's aircraft at 350, tanks at 3,000, helicopters at 450 and heavy artillery pieces at 15,000. After defeat Iraq's army was estimated at 400,000 troops[19] reduced from 1 million, with its fifty-six divisions reduced by one-half.[20]

In sum, in comparison with either Saudi Arabia or Iraq, Iran's military expenditures and arms imports have been modest. Its military capabilities have been reduced both in comparison to its own force levels in 1979 and in relation to its much smaller neighbors, whose inventories have grown. Although defeated and weakened by sanctions, Iraq still has superiority over Iran in all categories of major weapons systems. Saudi Arabia, with a population with one-quarter the size of Iran's, has more combat aircraft than Iran. Compared with the baseline year of 1979 and the inventory inherited from the Shah, trends in military capability and balance have shifted against revolutionary Iran.

FOCUSES OF EFFORTS IN ARMS PROCUREMENT PROGRAMS

In attempting to accurately assess Iran's acquisitions one must treat "unconfirmed reports" and the speculation and extrapolation often accompanying them with some skepticism. This is an area where there are few hard facts; agreements tend to be protracted and are often postponed or canceled without fanfare; deliveries do not translate quickly into operational capability, since assimilation is a lengthy process. Several factors limit Iran's buildup, the most important of which is diminishing resources. The latest estimates suggest arms expenditures of $800 million in 1993, down from annual levels of $2 billion to $3 billion in preceding years.[21] Other factors limiting the scope and effectiveness of Iran's arms acquisition program are, in summary: divisions within Iran's military; the lack of trained technicians, pilots and other skilled personnel; the variety of equipment, complicating maintenance; uncertainty regarding supplies;

Table 5   ESTIMATES OF ARMS DELIVERIES TO AND AGREEMENTS WITH SELECTED MIDDLE EAST COUNTRIES, 1988-91

	SIPRI (major deliveries)	CRS (arms deliveries)	CRS (arms agreements)
Egypt	—	—	$8.3 billion
Iran	$2.2 billion	$7.5 billion	10.5
Iraq	5.2	9.6	—
Israel	2.2	—	—
Saudi Arabia	8.6	28.9	37.0

Figures are estimates in billions of 1992 dollars. The SIPRI figures are estimates of deliveries of major arms. Adapted from table six in *Limiting Conventional Arms Exports to the Middle East* (U.S. Congress: Congressional Budget Office, September, 1992). Sources include the *1992 SIPRI Yearbook; World Armament and Disarmament* (New York: Oxford University Press, 1992); and Richard Grimmet, *Conventional Arms Transfer to the Third World, 1984-91* (Congressional Research Service, July 1992).

the attempt to switch sources and types of equipment; the absence of significant domestic production capability despite frequent claims; and the attempt to rebuild and modernize across the board, which puts great strain on resources, both human and financial.

Iran's effort to rebuild is starting from a low base, especially compared with its neighbors.[22] Its arms imports reflect its priorities. In rebuilding, its first area of focus has been arms for the regular military, emphasizing unit strength over numbers. By 1992 its tank force had shrunk to about 750 from 1,735 in 1979. Hence it has sought to enhance its armor and artillery from Russia and Czechoslovakia. It has favored specialized independent brigades over infantry divisions, it has displayed a tendency to modernize armor and artillery and to mechanize where possible. Nevertheless, its ground forces are handicapped by the mix of equipment, an ineffective logistical and command system and the lack of training exercises to teach maneuver warfare and combined arms exercises.

THE AIR FORCE

A second area of focus, the air force, has similar problems. It emerged from the war with only a one-quarter of its prewar stocks intact. Those aircraft that are still nominally operational are mainly U.S.-made, and their reliability and effectiveness are in doubt. Due to lack of supplies and maintenance, their avionics, radar and missile systems may not be operational at all. Since 1988, manpower for the air force and air defense has been rebuilt to between 25,000 and 35,000 but there remains a shortage of pilots and technicians. To augment capabilities Iran has shifted to Soviet (and then to Russian) sources of supply. Building on an agreement made in June 1989, Iran gained an unexpected gift of Soviet aircraft when Iraqi pilots fled their country in 1991.[23] Iran is taking delivery of thirty to forty Mig-29's (of fifty ordered from Russia) and some eighteen to thirty-six Su-24's (ordered in 1989 and possibly increased in 1991). These first-line aircraft together with support equipment and training will enable Iran to begin to rebuild the air force and make the switch to this new source. The Mig-29's are a modern air superiority/escort with air-to-air missiles and deep penetration capability. The Su-24's have a long range, reaching 790 to 1,600 kilometers. "With extended range fuel tanks and airborne refueling, the Su-24 can reach virtually any target in Iraq and the southern gulf."[24]

There are unconfirmed reports that Iran since 1991 had ordered from both Russia and China some seventy-two F-7 fighters, twenty-five Su-24's, fifty Mig-29's and a number of Su-37's (and two hundred T-72 tanks).[25] Major orders from these sources and support have allegedly increased air power by some 40 percent also making the aircraft obtained from Iraq operational.[26] Some sources report that Iran is due to receive a dozen TU-22M (Backfire) supersonic bombers. This would make Iran the only country in the region with modern strategic bombers whose unrefueled combat radius would cover the entire Middle East and beyond that to South Asia, Southeast and Central Europe and the Horn of Africa. If these reports are true (which appears highly unlikely) some analysts suggest that within two years Iran will have an air force four hundred planes strong—larger than any other state's in the region.[27] In fact, however, there is no indication of any new agreement since 1989. Iran has received no more than forty Mig-29's total and twenty to thirty Su-24's (together with twelve F-7 aircraft from China and upgraded Scuds from Korea).[28]

It is instructive to note that not all Iranian officials are happy about the switch from U.S. to Russian arms, let alone to Chinese-made ones. There are few illusions that it is a step forward. Defense Minister Akbar Torkan referred wistfully to the supply of parts for aircraft from the United States as Iran's principal arms problem. He said that the U.S.-supplied F-14 was "the best air superiority fighter that money can buy. In the next twenty years nothing will be its competitor. For close support we have the F-5's and for deep strikes F-4 fighters, this is a very good configuration." He added that Iran's air transport and helicopter fleets were all U.S.-made and that Iran's priority was to find parts "in order to keep them flying." The low-performance Chinese F-7 aircraft purchases he characterized unenthusiastically as intended "to fulfill the number of flight hours our pilots must have."[29]

With time, if Iran masters the Russian aircraft and supplies continue, it will have the nucleus of a new air force to replace its U.S. aircraft. These latter cannot remain operational for much longer. The Chinese F-7's have proven difficult to service and are unlikely to be continued.

Iran's air defense is a shambles, old or virtually nonexistent. The principal Western supplied systems are nonoperational; the I-Hawk, of which thirty remain, is, of dubious value. Iran has lost its warning and air control capacity. With little or no maintenance of radar since 1979 and few qualified operators, ground-based defense is rudimentary. This has led one observer to conclude that Iran has "only minimal capacity to fight a large-scale war or maintain an effective air defense system."[30]

There are unconfirmed reports of purchases of C5A-I radar systems from Russia, SA-10/SA-12 heavy SAM anti-theater ballistic missile systems and a new model of an early-warning command and control system. Given the example of Iraq's fate, Iran would certainly have a powerful incentive to put a high priority on missile detection. If the reports are true, this capability would enable Iran to rebuild the ground-based defense and early-warning sensor system and greatly improve the air forces's command and control system.[31]

THE NAVY

The comparison between Iran's navy in 1979 and 1988 is much the same as for the air force. Under the Shah the navy was developed for missions beyond coastal defense. It had ordered or taken delivery of through-deck cruisers for vertical/stationary takeoff and landing aircraft (V/STOL craft like the Harrier jump jet), submarines from Germany (six IKL-209) and a dozen P-3F Orion land-based maritime surveillance aircraft. It ordered six state-of-the-art Spruance-class destroyers (later reduced to four), but these were never delivered because of the revolution. Even before the hostage crisis poisoned relations with the United States and ended the arms-supply link, the new government had canceled some $10.6 billion worth of outstanding arms orders.[32] Iran thus had a potent navy for coastal defense and was developing a modest but (by regional standards) impressive blue-water ocean-going capability.

Recent events have accentuated the sense of the Persian Gulf's vulnerability and hence the priority attached to its security. During exchanges with the United States in 1987-88, Iran's navy was battered; U.S. forces sank a corvette, two minesweepers and several guided-missile frigates; they damaged two destroyers and destroyed Iran's oil-production platforms. In 1987-88, an allied naval presence threatened to blockade Iran if it did not agree to U.N.-stipulated terms to end the war with Iraq. Barely three years later, in 1990-91, another allied flotilla of ships entered the Gulf and imposed a blockade on Iraq.

In addition to the security threat posed by these episodes is the economic reality that the Gulf is the route for all of Iran's oil exports (hence a key link in the flow of foreign exchange revenues) and most of its trade. Moreover Iran's oil fields and installations are located around the waterway and are vulnerable to hostile incursions from the south. This economic dependence combined with past defense lessons reinforces Iran's determination to rebuild its naval forces with three principal goals:

- defense of the approaches to the Persian Gulf and Gulf of Oman;

- defense of its own coastal areas; and

- protection and defense of its own shipping.

For the present, Iran's naval capacity remains limited. It remains basically a coastal defense force. Its missions revolve around the following:

- deterrence of an active presence by an outside power in the region; this could be a non-Gulf power like India as well as the United States;

- deterrence of easy riskless intervention by outside powers in a regional crisis; and

- development of a capability to monitor and track shipping and to deny sea-control to outside powers.

The current naval buildup is an attempt to reconstruct a shattered service whose equipment is in dire need of modernization. Today there is no sign that Iran intends to acquire an ocean-going component comparable with what it had in 1979, while the land-based air arm of maritime operations is much reduced.

Since 1988 Tehran has sought to rebuild the navy using existing equipment where possible. As with the air force's air defense, much of the navy's radar and solid state equipment for communications, fire control and so forth are in disrepair and its seaborne missiles are of dubious value operationally speaking. In addition, the navy has lost much of its trained manpower over the course of the revolution and war.

Nevertheless Iran is still the region's dominant naval power, less subject to manpower constraints than the other Gulf states or to problems of access like Iraq. The navy now comprises 15,000 members of the regular military and 20,000 sailors from the Revolutionary Guard. While it can operate its approximately eighty remaining vessels, which include three destroyers, five frigates, fast attack craft and hovercraft, the navy's capacity for effective operation remains doubtful. And without extensive refit these Western-supplied ships will soon be unusable.

The pattern of Iran's naval rebuilding program is a notable indicator of probable defense strategies. It has not sought to replace or add to its holdings of larger ships (destroyers, frigates and the like). It has focused instead on weapons that might deny control of the Persian Gulf to an interventionary force. It is reported to have a significant stock of Mark-65 mines, Soviet AMD-500 mines, and AMAG-1 KRAB antiship mines (perhaps Chinese versions of Soviet mines). Iran also claims to have produced its own nonmagnetic acoustic free-floating mines. Such weapons could be used to deter intervention and slow naval penetration of the Gulf by outside forces.

A second category of weapon which Iran has sought to acquire is the Kilo-class submarine, two of which had been delivered by Russia by September 1993 out of three on order. The third Kilo-class submarine is due to be delivered in the spring of 1994. Originally ordered in mid-1989 when Iraq still occupied Iranian territory, the submarines were intended to counter the imminent delivery of six frigates to Iraq from Italy. The submarines were delivered in a new context, after Desert Storm had reduced the urgency of the Iraqi threat. Iranian officials now justified them as a necessary component of a balanced navy.[33] It is likely that Iran will also take possession of several minisubmarines from Russia.

A number of issues about the Kilos remain. First is their intended basing—inside the Gulf (at Bandar Abbas) or outside (at Chah Behar) where a port has yet to be built. Second, the operation of the subs with a fifty-two man crew will require training and improvements in command and control. Third, Iran's intentions are unclear: the submarines cannot easily be envisaged on missions inside the Gulf or against local Gulf powers. They appear intended for sea denial and defense of territorial waters. Like the mines the submarines appear to reflect lessons derived from the experience of the 1980s, when intervention by foreign fleets in the Gulf met with no serious opposition and Iran's naval and oil assets were exposed. Mines and submarines make future interventions more risky and complicated. Thus the Kilo-class subs provide Iran with a mode of operating in the Gulf environs in which its vulnerability to air and surface attacks is reduced.[34] The Kilos also have a mine-laying capability, making it harder for an intervention force to advance.

Missiles are a third area of emphasis for the navy. Iran has received sixty to one hundred C-801 (or YF-6) missiles. This is a short-range (70 kilometer/42 mile) antiship missile that can be launched from ships, land or aircraft. The Revolutionary Guard, whose naval functions appear to have been augmented, control the CSS-2 Silkworm antiship missiles. This is a copy of the Soviet Styx with a 450-kilogram (990-pound) warhead and a range of 80 to 90 kilometers (48 to 54 miles). The Guard probably has some fifty to sixty missiles and three or four operational launchers. Revolutionary Guard forces are stationed at island bases and oil platforms and at the main port of Bandar Abbas. The Silkworm missiles are deployed near the Straits of Hormuz as well as farther north in the Gulf. The Guard's navy (in theory under the same commander as the regular navy) controls the fast Swedish patrol boats and has a naval infantry detachment. The Guard may also have another Chinese antiship missile, the C-801.[35]

Iran's naval exercises stress amphibious operations characterized by rapid attacks by fast patrol boats with air cover. In large-scale exercises lasting more than ten days in 1992 and 1993, naval forces practiced blocking the straits and liberating islands; they covered a large area with some 45 surface ships, 150 small craft and an unspecified number of aircraft.[36] The scale of these operations, Iran's strategic assets (its manpower pool and long coastline) and the sustained buildup of Iran's naval forces generate anxiety among its smaller neighbors. Naval power need not be visible to have influence; even if held back, the latent threat of naval intervention could inhibit or intimidate Iran's neighbors. If Iran continues its naval buildup, especially by adding more missiles to its inventory or expanding its limited amphibious capability (currently enough to move about eight hundred to nine hundred troops and twenty-five to thirty-five tanks), its neighbors' suspicions about its ultimate intentions will surely increase.

What does its arms program suggest about Iran's intentions? An Iranian military rebuilding effort is inevitable and logical given the scale of losses, the difficult neighborhood in which it lives and Iran's will to play some role there. Its pace has picked up but Iran will have difficulty sustaining it. The particulars of the program are unsurprising, the replacement of aircraft (and armor) for example. The inclination to get the best aircraft available (long-range Su-24's and Mig-29's) is understandable since Iran is a large country. The scope of the program is not extravagant and has built-in limitations. However particular weapons systems and capabilities have caused concern. Antiship missiles, submarines and mines appear to be intended for a sea-denial mission aimed at deterring a repetition of the events of 1987-88, that is at outside powers rather than Gulf powers. Long-range missiles and weapons of mass destruction are another matter entirely, worrisome to both local and outside powers.

MISSILES AND WEAPONS OF MASS DESTRUCTION

Iraq's surprise use of missiles and chemical weapons, which proved politically and psychologically devastating, found Iran exposed, diplomatically isolated and without a countervailing deterrent. These assaults galvanized Tehran's resolve to seek these classes of weapons. There has been no break in its search for equivalent capabilities across the board; the revelations about Iraqi programs made after Desert Storm have only intensified this quest.

In the missile exchanges of the war of the cities Iran had fewer and shorter-range missiles. Iraq had adapted the Scud to develop the Al-Husayn missile with a range of some 400 to 500 kilometers/240 to 300 miles and a heavier warhead. Despite its 1991 defeat Iraq still poses a potential missile threat to its neighbors.[37] This would increase if it were to break out of the current arms control regime imposed by the United Nations, which limits it to missiles with a maximum range of 150 kilometers (90 miles) (versus the Missile Technology Control Regime's 300 kilometers/180 miles).

Iran has sought an enhanced missile capability since 1987. One approach it has employed has been developing indigenous missiles. Despite the high priority assigned to it, the results have not been impressive. The first, the Oghab, a Chinese type-83 artillery rocket, is an inaccurate counter-city weapon (range: 40 kilometers/24 miles; circular error probable—CEP: 1,000 meters/3,200 feet). The second, Nazeat (Iran-130), is inaccurate and unreliable in service (maximum range: 90-120 kilometers/54-72 miles). The third, Shahin-2 with a 180 kilogram (396-pound) conventional warhead, chemical warhead or submunitions, weighs 580 kilograms (1,276 pounds). It is difficult to resist the conclusion that Iran's poor results are due to deficiencies of organization and management (rather than backwardness in technology), a factor that would have ramifications for Iran's ambitious defense reconstruction programs across the board.[38]

The missile most used has been the imported Scud-B, with a range of 290 to 310 kilometers (174 to 186 miles) and a 1,000 kilo (2,200 pound) warhead. This has been in the inventory since 1985 and Iranian purchases from North Korea have reportedly continued since 1988. Some experts put Iran's holdings as of mid-1992 at two hundred fifty to three hundred Scud-Bs and fifteen to thirty launchers.[39] There are also reports of a longer range (500-600 kilometer/300-360 mile) improved Scud-C developed by North Korea, ordered by Mohsen Rezai of the Pasdaran and delivered in mid-1991. Iran is reported to have test-fired this version and now to have perhaps twenty to thirty of them. Iran and Syria are suspected of cooperating with North Korea and each other in the development of the Scud-C. Iran is also believed to be seeking the more accurate M-family of missiles from China, either the M-9 or M-11.[40] Iran is due to receive the long-range No-Dong missile (1,000 kilometers/600 miles). Recently developed and test-fired by North Korea, Iran may be seeking to produce as well as acquire this missile.

Iran thus seeks to build its own missiles while acquiring the most capable missiles available abroad. It seeks the broadest technology transfer where possible and enters into cooperative agreements with suppliers and other recipients. In its quest for missiles it has solidified its arms relationships with North Korea and China, which stemmed from its urgent search for new supply sources during the war with Iraq. Today the relationship is still more commercial than strategic; but since the suppliers are states considered unfriendly, dangerous or alien to the West and its values, it reinforces the image of Iran as irresponsible and threatening.

From Iraqi chemical attacks Iran learned the necessity of confronting potential users with an equivalent capability to deter them. Shortly after Desert Storm, an Iranian official alleged that the USSR, Turkey, Afghanistan and the U.S. Navy had access to chemical weapons and that Iran "reserves the right...to get the technological know-how to confront the chemical agents our enemies might use against us." He put equal emphasis on "studying ways of averting the use of chemical weapons and neutralizing their effects."[41] These comments reflected a shift in emphasis—it was not just Iraq that posed this threat but others as well; it was thus a preemptive bid to justify Iran's continued interest in chemical weaponry.

Iranian military exercises routinely encompass possible chemical weapons attacks by enemies, while official statements deny any intention of developing a chemical weapons capability. Iran stresses the moral considerations involved: "It is not acceptable under any circumstances," Rafsanjani has stated, "to harm humanity by means of nuclear weapons or any other means of mass destruction, such as chemical weapons and such like."[42]

Iran quickly accepted the Chemical Weapons Convention in 1993, though after much initial skepticism. In 1990 Iran's foreign minister, Akbar Velayati, indicated that Iran would sign a comprehensive convention but thought that the chances of it being honored by all the states in the Persian Gulf (that is, by Iraq) "were somewhere near zero."[43] Desert Storm gave added impetus to the convention and it was quickly concluded. Iran was unenthusiastic about the new momentum. It stressed the importance of controlling challenge inspections to guard against their frivolous or malicious use against particular states. To discourage such use as well as veiled "fishing" expeditions designed for espionage, Iran proposed that challenging states should be liable for the costs of inspections. It pushed for the creation of an executive council to review challenges and sought membership for Third World states or nations friendly to itself on that council.

Iran also emphasized the need to assure continued technology transfer: "The industries of the Third World should not be threatened under the pretext of chemical weapons disarmament."[44] Judging from similar statements by states opposed to the convention (China, Cuba, India and Pakistan), This tack was as much a debating stance to gain the votes of the developing states as a reflection of genuine concern.

Nevertheless, Iran has signed the treaty, under which it accepts inspections whose intrusiveness is unparalleled in previous arms control agreements. Unlike Egypt, Syria and others it did not link adherence to the treaty to Israel's compliance with the Nuclear Nonproliferation Treaty. It may find other ways around the treaty. It could delay or not ratify the treaty. It might wait for other states to raise objections about its implementation and make common cause on such issues as the interpretation of permissible activities or it might allege discriminatory behavior by the Australia Group suppliers.[45] Alternatively it might ratify the treaty and count on the fact that chemical (and biological) weapons raw materials are accessible, cheaper and widely available because of their industrial applications. This makes it difficult to track them, or to interfere with the acquisition of the components that go into chemical and biological weapons. Inspections could be undermined by a similar handicap. Hence Iran's ratification need not entail certain compliance. By creating a presumption of compliance it would make aggressive detection and inspection harder.

Suspicions about Iran's intentions are increased by the pattern of activity outside the realm of public diplomacy. Since 1988 scattered, repeated reports have surfaced of Iran's efforts to obtain materials necessary for chemical weapons.[46] The case in July-August 1993 of a Chinese freighter suspected of carrying chemical weapons precursors for Iran—which was not proven—is only the latest and most public of a long list of such episodes.[47] U.S. officials are clear about Iran's military intentions though not about the precise state of actual capabilities. The CIA has reported that Iran's chemical weapons program has expanded since 1988 and though still "relatively crude" it is "extensive and improving." The CIA also expects Iran to develop chemical warheads for its missiles within a few years, and suspects it of working to acquire a "biological warfare capability."[48]

More specifically Iran's program allegedly includes mustard gas, blood and nerve agents, and bombs and artillery shells filled with these agents. The amounts involved (according to CIA Director Robert Gates) could be between "several hundred and 2,000 tons of blister, choking and blood agents."[49] The most recent reports from the same sources confirm the trend: Iran's defense effort "includes a serious, determined program to develop all categories of weapons of mass destruction." Iran is reported to have an "active chemical and biological weapons program" and to have stockpiled chemical weapons.[50] Iran is active in biological weapons as well. Iran is rumored to have been working on mycotoxins since the early 1980s. Its attempts to purchase two tell-tale strains of fungus seem to have confirmed this. It is known to be doing research on anthrax and in the area of biotoxins and may be working to produce bacteriological weapons at a pesticide facility near Tehran. In general information about the volume of production and progress in weaponization is not known. Most observers agree that Iran's quest for missiles is directly related to its chemical (and nuclear) weapons program, that is for delivery of those weapons.[51]

What are Iran's intentions? On the face of it, Iraq's capabilities provide Iran with a continuing incentive to gird itself. CIA Director James Woolsey has noted that "neither war nor inspections have seriously degraded" Iraq's biological warfare program.[52] Scenarios of renewed conflict are not far-fetched: Iraq may evade U.N. controls and seek a war of revenge against its neighbor; another regime may replace Saddam Hussein's, dilute the controls and continue with its chemical and biological arms programs. In any case Iran, given its experience, is not willing to rely on the United States or United Nations to come to its defense. In these circumstances maintenance of a capability to retaliate in kind to establish a deterrent may be prudent.

Other than this, it is difficult to see any concrete uses: these are not weapons of choice against secessionist movements nor practical instruments to pass on to terrorists. Apart from their assumed use as a general retaliatory deterrent they have no specific value. Iran's own incentives fall into Brad Roberts' category of "no immediate strategic purpose."[53]

The limited and specific conditions under which chemical weapons (and biological weapons) are effective militarily, the international norms being established to prevent their acquisition (as well as their use) and the narrow range of contingencies in which their use or threatened use are rewarding argue against the value of this category of weapon. Such arguments have not persuaded the leadership in Tehran, however, which prefers to put its faith in its own capabilities. One element impelling it toward such a policy is its perception that the United States is a hostile power against which it needs to have many options. Chemical weapons and missiles might discourage pressure from outside powers or their reflexive involvement in regional affairs.

NUCLEAR TECHNOLOGY OR WEAPONS?

The pace of nuclear proliferation globally has been a function of political will rather than technological capability. With the inexorable diffusion of technology and the globalization of knowledge, the physics involved in the construction of nuclear weapons is no longer a limiting factor. Cost is not a primary consideration either; spread over time a crude weapon is not beyond the budget of most states. Access to weapons-grade fissile materials and weapons designers remain the principal bottlenecks, but even these are unlikely to do more than slow the determined proliferator. The decision to seek nuclear weapons turns above all on political criteria: on perceptions of a state's security in the prevailing international environment, its objectives and goals and the contribution that a nuclear capability can make to them. This section assesses these dimensions of the question, leaving aside detailed discussion of Iran's current capability.[54]

Since 1988 Iran has invested much effort in reviving its stalled nuclear program, first by trying to persuade Germany to finish its two half-completed reactors in Bushire, then trying to convince other suppliers of its desire for cooperation in this domain. Due to U.S. pressure and Western alarm at the Iraqi experience, no other suppliers have been forthcoming and Iran has consequently decided on cooperation with China and Russia. The latter are more willing to accept Iran's assurances about its intentions, and the nuclear cooperation agreements they have concluded, which include safeguards, are compatible with the obligations of both supplier and recipient set forth in the Nuclear Nonproliferation Treaty (NPT).

Iran has insisted that as a party to the NPT it has a right to obtain nuclear technology for peaceful purposes. It depicts efforts at controlling or limiting this as an attempt to impede the growth of developing countries.[55] Iran states that its efforts to develop a nuclear industry are motivated by the need for a larger power generation capacity and the desire to develop expertise in such wide ranging applications as medicine, agriculture and industry. Iranian officials argue that access to atomic energy is "the right of all nations" and that Iranian technicians need to familiarize themselves with this technology. They contend that, "If we do not use the current generation of nuclear power plants, we will not be able at all to use the next generation of these plants."[56] As proof of their peaceable intent Iranian officials point to their adherence to the NPT and their sponsorship of a proposal to create a nuclear-weapons-free zone.[57]

Iran sees current U.S. nonproliferation policy as discriminatory, selective and unilateralist. Washington, in this view, is treating the Iraqi case as typical and putting the onus on states signatory to the NPT to prove that they are *not* cheating. Furthermore it is targeting only certain states, such as Iran, while ignoring egregious nonsignatories, such as Israel. It is also seeking to prevent the transfer of *any* nuclear technology to these states, despite the explicit recognition of their right of access to technologies for peaceful uses given in Article 4 of the NPT, which was a condition of many states' adherence (and part of the famous "package deal").

The United States's position is clear: proliferation among the NPT signatories is as much a problem as among nonsignatories; the transfer of any nuclear technology that improves the training of technicians and familiarizes them with materials that could be diverted or become the basis of a weapons program is to be stopped; and the United States and its allies should focus on certain high-risk states early enough to make a difference in their programs, however rudimentary their current capacity.[58]

In the Iranian view the Iraqi case is being used as an excuse for the continuation of a vendetta against Iran, a pretext for continuing to deny it technology and to discriminate against it. President Rafsanjani pointed to U.S. pressure on other states intended to stop technology "even for non-military purposes."[59] Iranian officials say that Iran has "not been treated fairly" on this subject. Discrimination against Iran is contrasted with U.S. indulgence of Israel which "has 200 bombs at its disposal" and has not signed the NPT.[60] This blatantly selective approach, in Iran's view, characterizes all U.S. arms-control policies in the region. Hence their rejection of the May 1991 Bush proposal that sought to cap and freeze the transfer of fissile material without dealing with Israel's already existing nuclear stockpile. This double-standard with regard to the possession of nuclear weapons is especially irksome.[61] Since 1991, when Israel began to criticize Iran for its nuclear program and one official threatened under certain circumstances to deal with it, Iran has felt under particular pressure.[62]

Iran's nuclear program remains at a very preliminary stage, with a small research reactor operating and only tentative agreements on expansion. However the absence of pressing motivation for civil use, the pattern of proposed purchases, the scope of declared ambitions, the resources that Iran could invest in it and the size of the manpower pool to be dedicated to it have caused alarm.[63] Iran wants nuclear power to account for 10 to 20 percent of its energy needs. It plans to train some 450 technicians (with 250 "senior experts" already trained). Another 500 are to be trained in work study courses in Iran at the Nuclear Energy College at Bushire and abroad, probably Italy). Another 1,500 will be introduced to working with radiation for medical science. Iran has also invited Iranians abroad to return and contribute to the nuclear energy program.[64]

Iran is said to have given unmistakable signs of going beyond a peaceful program, of seeking a weapons capability and of considering "whether to go the enrichment route or the plutonium route."[65] Hence the U.S. view that any technology transfers, because of the overlap, would contribute toward a weapons program; though still some eight to ten years from completion it can be delayed by strict controls of materials from advanced states. This time scale is not universally held.[66]

The state of Iran's program is thus ambiguous: ambitious but rudimentary with a claimed emphasis on peaceful uses contradicted by assessments of weapons intentions.[67] Iran's statements about nuclear weapons are equally opaque. Iran's leaders no longer openly call for the development of nuclear weapons as Rafsanjani did in 1988: "[We] should fully equip ourselves both in the offensive and defensive use of chemical, bacteriological and radiological weapons." Today Iran denies any such intention but does so with faint conviction, pointing to problems with the current situation which cannot last. Two examples suffice. In 1990 President Rafsanjani told Hans Blix, director of the International Atomic Energy Agency, that while nuclear weapons were a bad thing, nuclear energy was important. However, he went on, as long as one state armed with nuclear weapons existed, control was impossible. The mere signing of a ban on nuclear weapons was not enough. In light of the existence of missiles and Iran's experience with Iraq, it was evident that whenever the vital interests of states were threatened, they would not "obey international regulations."[68]

An Iranian newspaper editorial captured this ambivalence, arguing that nuclear weapons would only detract from the security of proliferating states but that in their quest for security ("the new lawless international political environment is a terrifying place") states would inevitably be driven toward "the necessity of possessing a national deterrent such as a nuclear bomb." This was because of the weakness or absence of rules and laws, and the tendency of some powerful states to apply arbitrary double standards and discriminate against the weaker states.[69]

Statements by other figures, whether official or personal, reflect a similar ambivalence. These are usually couched in terms of Iran's right to obtain nuclear weapons as long as Israel has them.[70] Other senior figures have emphasized the impracticality or immorality of nuclear weapons. Maj. Gen. Ali Shabazi, Chief of the Joint Staffs, said: "We believe war with nuclear weapons is a war against humanity and for the same reason we have never sought to acquire or build such weapons."[71] Spiritual Leader Khamenei: "[even] if it were the case that the Islamic Republic of Iran wanted to make an atomic bomb, the big powers [would still] have hundreds of them." Still, "That which gives strength to a system is not the atomic bomb."[72] Iran is however convinced that access to technology and equipment as well as modern science are essential components of national security, and is determined to achieve this.[73]

What does all this say about the attitude of Iran's current leaders toward nuclear weapons? The evidence is fragmentary, indirect and inconclusive in statements and policies. Yet in sum it is consistent with a view that Iran is a serious candidate for nuclear weapons acquisition.

Iran's view of the world and its own role are the strongest motivants for acquiring nuclear weapons. Seen from Tehran a unipolar world in which the U.S. wields unchallenged prominence, controlling the U.N., dictating supplier cartels, selling and restricting arms and technology at will, is a dangerous place. Iran's sense of encirclement feeds into its fears of fragmentation and of hostile powers' attempts to promote its disintegration. Isolated and increasingly discriminated against by the United States and its allies, Tehran sees—or at least depicts—its economic and political problems as the costs of behaving "independently."

Against this tableau of constraint and vulnerability is Iran's conception of its own role, regional and global. It is the foremost Muslim state promoting "true" (as opposed to "American") Islam, taking stands on Islamic issues while globally "present," "striving" against oppression. Iran's definition of its mission requires not just will but resources. It needs access to technology, arms, credits and markets.

A strong and unstable mixture of grievance and ambition colors Iran's international outlook, and fuels its policies. The sense of discrimination, of not being respected, of seeking equality, demanding of Washington "recognition" of the revolution, animates this regime. This sense of aggrievement and ambition are a search for status, which is compatible with the argument other states (namely France and the United Kingdom) made to justify their decisions to acquire nuclear weapons. In Iran's case the "table" argument is a strong motivation in a regime that feels neglected and self-important. Several other subsidiary motives are consistent with Iran's values.

- Self-reliance as a value would be achieved—and seem to be achieved—in quintessential form by nuclear weapons.

- Nuclear weapons would serve as a symbol of the revolution's success before a domestic audience; in this respect they could divert attention from the failure to deliver economic prosperity.

- Nuclear weapons would emphatically symbolize Iran's technological progress.

- Nuclear weapons could bridge the widening gap between the conventional military capabilities of advanced and less advanced states.

- Nuclear weapons could reduce the cost of defense and the importance of conventional weapons which are expensive and hard to master, maintain and replace.

- Nuclear weapons could provide Iran with a leading role in regional politics, from which it has been increasingly marginalized and risks becoming even more so.

- Nuclear weapons would amplify Iran's international voice, which is essential if the revolution is to be taken seriously.

If Iran is seeking to acquire nuclear weapons it would be in keeping with its style to deny it—to avoid confrontation, to envelope its motives in discussions about industry and technology and to position its own case within that of a class of developing states interested in unhindered technology transfers. Its approach would be by indirection and deception; it would avoid a more detectable "crash program," inviting unhindered inspections and accepting safeguards while counting on its ability to slip through the cracks of inspections and international bureaucracy and the ambiguities of "dual use," whether in nuclear or chemical and biological areas. Here the United States aids Iran's subterfuge: the more hostile and selective the United States is in its attitude toward Iran, the more Tehran can depict U.S. accusations as punitive and distorted, motivated by hostility. In this way Iran may even seek to undermine the motivation behind U.S. intelligence which is critical in the new inspection systems for chemical and nuclear weapons detection.

What would the military motives be for an Iranian bomb? It seems clear that military considerations are not paramount, for Iran is not engaged in a race against a specific enemy. However there is a risk of an Iraqi re-emergence at some future date, which could be followed by a quick resumption of its nuclear program. A second motive could be to deter a U.S. intervention against the regime or Iran's vital interests; such a capability could give the United States pause. A third motive lies in the need for a general hedge in a region that is becoming nuclearized in part from the north.

The coercive uses of nuclear weapons do not appear preeminent in Iran's calculations. These might include attempts at intimidating its neighbors to cause them to sever their ties with the United States, or gaining better terms in OPEC from the Saudis. Compellence against non-nuclear Iraq is possible. Threats against Turkey, a NATO member, appear remote. Conceptions of actual use appear even more distant. The unsolved problems of targeting and delivery; the threat of retaliation; the problems of collateral damage and international reactions; the moral dimensions as well as the "style" of the Iranian leadership to date make acquisition for use a most unlikely motive. However it is possible that misjudgment could give rise to an escalation from the symbolic dimension of having the bomb to use in anger.

Notwithstanding the equivocal declarations and uncertainties about the intentions behind its civil program, there is an affinity between Iran's goals and needs and the search for a nuclear weapons capability. As with chemical weapons this capability would be consistent with its aim of self-reliance, and it would tend to affirm its stature, which is so important to Iran's sense of mission as a role model for Islamic revolution. The experience and lessons of the past fifteen years seen from the vantage of today's hostile environment reinforce the conclusion for Iran that chemical, biological and nuclear weapons are necessary and prudent hedges for the future of the Islamic Republic.

IMPACT ON REGIONAL AND INTERNATIONAL SECURITY

Iran's arms buildup reflects an intention to fulfill what it considers its geographically and ideologically determined role of dominant power in the Persian Gulf. This claim has a shriller edge to it now that it has been resisted by its neighbors and has proved more elusive. Iran justifies its buildup accordingly. "As the smaller countries around us have armed themselves to the teeth and buy the most modern war material, we too—as a big and vast country which has been the target of many threats throughout history and especially during the decade of the Islamic revolution—will do the same...."[1]

Iran's arms programs will stimulate further military efforts by the Arab states of the Gulf, independently increasing tension in the region. With Iraq temporarily eclipsed, the threat for them from Iran looms large in the Gulf, to the extent that Iran's territorial differences with one Arab state (the United Arab Emirates) are seen as evidence of wider territorial ambitions.[2] The broader question that remains, however, is whether Iran's military reconstruction will increase the regime's ambitions and its scope for miscalculation. Or, more specifically, what impact will the buildup have on Iran's attitude towards the use of force in its relations with Iraq, its Gulf neighbors, vis-à-vis the United States (especially in the Gulf) and toward Israel?

IRAQ: PLANNING FOR RECURRENT ROUNDS OF CONFLICT

Iran's military programs will affect Iraq most immediately. Iraq is Iran's only territorially contiguous Arab neighbor. Their long war was followed by a cease-fire but no peace treaty. The possibility of future wars clearly shapes their arms programs. In the short term maintaining Iraq's territorial integrity is Iran's prime concern; in the longer term another round of conflict cannot be excluded. Assuming that both sides posses chemical weapons, mutual deterrence should operate. In a future war missiles could figure more prominently. Even with relatively short ranges, missiles are potentially effective; Iraq's most significant targets militarily speaking are within 180 miles of Iran.[3] Furthermore a new round would bring with it intensified damage; with greater missile stockpiles, each side could fire twenty or so missiles a day for a total of 1,000, making the earlier "war of the cities" resemble a slow-motion affair.[4]

Missiles have already had an impact on the region: Iraqi missiles spurred Iran's acquisitions, which encouraged Saudi purchases of weapons with a comparable retaliatory capability (see Table 6).[5] Essentially, once missiles are in one country's inventory, the quest for longer range and better accuracy is irresistible, stimulating a missile arms race in

Table 6   BALLISTIC MISSILES INVENTORIED OR ORDERED BY IRAN, IRAQ, ISRAEL, SAUDI ARABIA, 1993 [a]

	Missile	Producer	Range (kilometers)	CEP[b] (meters)	Status
Iran	CSS-N-1 (HY-2) Silkworm	People's Republic of China	80	n.a.	In service
	Iran-130, Nazeat, Mushak-120	Iran	120-130	n.a.	In service
	Mushak-160	Iran	160	n.a.	In service
	Iran-200 Mushak-200	Iran	200	n.a.	n.a.
	Scud-B (SS-1C)	USSR	280-320	500-1,600	In service
	Scud-C (SS-1D)	USSR	500-550	700-2,200	In service
	No-Dong 1 (Labour-1)	North Korea	1,000-1,300	"poor"	Development
	No-Dong 2	North Korea	1,000-2,000	n.a.	Development
	Tondar-68, M-18	People's Republic of China, Iran	1,000	n.a.	Development
	M-11 (DF-11)	People's Republic of China	300	n.a.	Development
	M-9 (DF-15)	People's Republic of China	600	300-700	Development
Iraq	Al- Husayn	Iraq	600-650	500-3,200	Terminated
	Al-Abbas	Iraq	900	3,000-4,800	Terminated
Israel	Jericho I	Israel	480-650	1,000-1,800	In service
	Jericho II	Israel	1,450-1,500	n.a.	In service
	Shavit	Israel	2,500 or 7,500	n.a.	In service
Saudi Arabia	CSS-2 (DF-3A)	People's Republic of China	2,000-2,800	1,200-2,000	In service

n.a.=not available
a. All figures include the range of numbers suggested by various sources.

b. CEP=circular error probable, the radius of a circle (from the target at the center) in which 50 percent of the missiles are expected to fall.

Sources: Arms Control Association, "The Proliferation of Ballistic Missiles," fact sheet, March 1, 1993; Joe Bermudez, "Ballistic Ambitions Ascendant," *Jane's Defence Weekly*, April 10, 1993, pp. 20-22; Anthony Cordesman, *Weapons of Mass Destruction in the Middle East* (London/Washington: Brassey's, 1991), 56-57; Duncan Lennox, *Jane's Strategic World Systems* (Alexandria, Va.: Jane's Information Group, 1990 [and looseleaf information updates through 1993]); Duncan Lennox, "Missile Race Continues," *Jane's Defence Weekly*, January 23, 1993, pp. 18-21; and Monterey Institute of International Studies, "Missile Capabilities of Selected Countries," *Missile Monitor*, Spring 1993.

the region. Parallel with it would be a race for theater anti-ballistic missile defense systems (Patriot, Arrow and their successors). There are signs of both kinds of contests in Iran's relations with it neighbors.

A related development is that missiles, with their longer reaches, tend to link conflict areas that had formerly been separate; this complicates defense planning, crisis management and arms control. As a result, the spread of missiles to the region has increased the vulnerability of all states. The primary characteristic of these missiles is a high probability of penetration, against which there is as yet little or no reliable defense, promising to increase damage if war occurs. As accuracy improves these weapons might have precise military objectives; for the moment they serve as a general deterrent or weapons that could be launched against cities for political effect.

The inaccuracy of missiles currently in stock, which makes them inefficient vehicles for delivering conventional warheads, gives rise to the presumption that they are intended for chemical, biological or nuclear armaments. The interaction between the assured penetration of missiles and weapons of mass destruction (both of which escalate terror but are of limited military utility) may tempt more states to start down the path toward nuclear weapons development. With the availability of missiles, "the road from a nuclear device to a nuclear weapon would be dramatically shortened."[6] This link has been demonstrated in the case of Iraq, and Iran now appears to have embarked on a similar course. The implication is that Iran's arms buildup in this area may deter Iraq but in the event of war will increase damage: in the meantime it contributes to the spiralling trend toward weapons of mass destruction in the region.

THE GULF STATES: COOPERATION OR DOMINATION?

The Arab states of the Persian Gulf, small and vulnerable in varying degrees, feel threatened by the very existence of Iran. Its revolutionary message and regional aspirations combined with its arms buildup increase their sense of insecurity. Some U.S. sources assume that Iran's arms programs will enable it dominate the region.[7] The implication is that this is what is intended. It is worth asking, however, what such domination would entail and whether Iran's military buildup makes this feasible. On the one hand, Iran will have the capacity to reach targets across the Gulf with its missiles. Long-range air power will also cover much of the region, though not unopposed and not in the short term. Iran's naval power cannot be challenged by the other littoral states without U.S. support. Iran's capacity to threaten shipping in the waterway is growing, especially with mines, submarines and coastal missiles. However, the political context in which this would be an Iranian objective remains unclear. Moreover, Iran's military programs have shown no marked emphasis on power projection capabilities. Iran is still unable to mount operations far from its borders. It has neither air- nor sea-lift and logistics for sustained operations distant from an Iranian home base. At best Iran has the capacity for "smash-and-grab" raids or harassing operations.

Missiles and weapons of mass destruction are another matter. They aggravate the sense of insecurity in the region given the vulnerability of city-states with nearby oil installations; they feed visions of apocalyptic destruction based on the ineluctable trend toward nuclearization. More immediately, they reinforce the estrangement between Iran and her neighbors. Missiles aside, how might Iran use military force?

Annexation. Annexation of territory is unlikely; Iran is not territorially revisionist and has no irredenta or claims. Its only contested land border, with Iraq (which was more a pretext than a cause of conflict), is temporarily settled. Its differences with the Gulf states are not primarily over territory. Annexation of islands or oil and gas fields are theoretically possible but counterproductive. The scenario of a "resource grab" like Saddam Hussein's some time in the future cannot, nevertheless, be totally discounted. If economic conditions in Iran deteriorate to such an extent that a foreign diversion is needed, a desperate act might ensue. But after Desert Storm this appears less probable.

Coercion. Iran's military power could in theory be used to intimidate and compel its smaller neighbors to accept its dominance of the region, to sever ties with the United States, to bow to its ultimatums on oil policy and so forth. Tehran's efforts at intimidation in the 1980s backfired, and the Arab states funded Iraq and supported the internationalization of the war. Since Desert Storm these states are more open in their ties to the United States, more reassured about its will, and with new arms, more confident about their own ability to manage threats. Iran would find it difficult to intimidate these states even after a major arms buildup over several years.

Subversion or a more subtle use of power. Intra-Arab disputes (such as between Bahrain and Qatar or Saudi Arabia and Qatar/Yemen) and internal stresses (succession problems, democratization, sectarian difficulties) may render certain Gulf states vulnerable domestically in the coming decade.

Iran may seek to exploit these weaknesses to expand its influence. In a civil war or coup it might take sides, even sponsoring rebellion. In none of these scenarios would Iran's military programs be a major factor, however, either in fomenting domestic strife or in its eventual outcome. Iran needs to assure and maximize its oil revenues in coming years. Policies threatening one's neighbors are not the most effective means of achieving this goal. Iran's military buildup does not change the prevailing political calculus. Its impact is therefore limited short of war.

THE UNITED STATES: DETERRENCE VERSUS ACCESS

While the United States insists on its right of access to the Persian Gulf, Iran feels threatened by its semipermanent presence in the region. Each state believes the other is animated by hostility. The United States is suspicious about Iran's intentions in the Persian Gulf. Iran's submarines, mines, air power and shore-based missiles could become a formidable threat to shipping in the Gulf. But it is easier to list Iran's inventory than to posit realistic scenarios in which Iran would have an interest in interrupting maritime traffic. It does have an interest, however, in seeing that the United States's ability to enter the Gulf is limited or constrained. For this purpose it need only create obstacles to unhindered access, creating inhibitions, rather than pose a serious threat.

The Iran-Iraq War showed that halting tanker traffic is more difficult than disrupting it. It would take many mines, torpedoes and missiles to constitute a severe or sustained impediment. Moreover Iran has vital interests in keeping the Gulf open for its own imports as well as exports. On closer examination, Iran's capability is not as impressive as if first seems: with three submarines, only one would be operational; and while it might not be detected, its base would be vulnerable to attack.[8] In addition, the Gulf's shallow waters are not ideally suited for submarine operations. Nevertheless Iranian submarines could lay mines requiring continuous surveillance and monitoring by the U.S. or allied forces to enable effective sweeping, all of which would inhibit and delay access and intervention in the Gulf.[9]

Hence, in combination with modernized coastal defenses Iran's arms buildup could pose problems for U.S. intervention in the Persian Gulf:[10]

- Iranian minelaying and submarine activity could impede and retard access by major ships to the Persian Gulf.

- A U.S. response to Iran would face different problems than it did in

Iraq. Iran's longer coastline and strategic depth would complicate defense planning and counterstrikes; U.S. maritime aircraft stationed outside the Gulf would require inflight refueling to reach targets in the upper Gulf or central Iran.

• A more complex threat environment would require better or more U.S. forces and greater U.S. commitment.

• The mixture of Iranian capabilities could become more troublesome than any particular weapon system. This could make a permanent land presence for U.S. forces more urgent and the need for a surge capacity a secondary consideration.

In sum, Iran's growing military capability cannot be readily translated into political influence with its neighbors. Its interests do not allow it to act recklessly. Iran's capability is undoubtedly a complicating factor for U.S. defense planners, however, making untrammelled access to the Persian Gulf less assured and riskier. Future weapons proliferation, of cruise missiles and the like will continue and reinforce this.

ISRAEL: NEW ADVERSARY OR SYMBOLIC FOE?

The reach of modern weapons systems, especially missiles, makes "security" a regional phenomenon and necessity. Iran's growing missile stocks, which are increasing in range (and in the future no doubt in accuracy), thus concern an Israel that was targeted by Iraqi missiles in the 1991 war. As with the Gulf states, the most important factor in Iran's arms buildup for Israel is its acquisition of weapons of mass destruction. There is no sign that Iran seeks a confrontation with Israel or that it is preparing for one. However, its policies and rhetoric have hardened. Iran singles out Israel to justify other states' right to have nuclear weapons. Israel in turn points to Iran's capabilities, actual and potential, as the reason for its own vigilance and preparedness.[11] But Israel's principal fear vis-à-vis Iran is political in nature: that an impasse in the peace process could give rise to an Islamicization of the dispute with Iran leading the way as chief spoiler, sponsor and sanctuary in reconstituting a new rejectionist front against Israel.

In such a context Iran's missile capability assumes importance. An extended-range missile like the No-Dong 1 which Iran is currently receiving from North Korea, has a 1,000-kilometer (600 mile) range and can reach Israel from Iran. Since Israel shares no common border with Iran, deterring it conventionally (as Israel does Syria) is not possible. Deterrence in this context is harder for Israel.[12] With the No-Dong 1 missile Iran could pose a substantial conventional threat to Israel in the near future; and in the longer term, as it marries nonconventional warheads to missiles, it could threaten Israel with weapons of mass destruction. In theory Iran's extended missiles would enable it to engage Israel without having a presence in a contiguous area. Missiles thus might enable Iran to leapfrog back into Middle Eastern politics even if it loses access to Lebanon, for which it depends on Syria. In the event that Damascus came to its own agreement with Israel parallel to the Palestinians and Jordan, how would Iran's react? Would Iran seek to sabotage these agreements and threaten Israel on a new front? Or would it hold fast to its missiles to deter any preventive Israeli strike, and back-peddle politically?

Politics in Iran today dictate a rejectionist position, but this will not be translated into a military commitment. Palestine remains a Muslim foreign policy issue; a stance on it is important for the regime's legitimacy but not essential for regime or national survival. Iran acquired missiles because of its experience in the war with Iraq; it was not motivated by a desire to confront Israel.

The danger today is not that Iran seeks to embark on a collision course with Israel but that increased capabilities together with changed political incentives may make such a confrontation possible or even likely later in the decade. The risk of such a development has influenced Prime Minister Rabin's approach to the Middle East.[13] It has united Egypt and Israel in that respect. Iran will have no nuclear capability before the end of the decade. By that time it will certainly have come to recognize that simply making a move toward these weapons, whatever the intent, unleashes forces and suspicions that no verbal denials or assurances can defuse. Iran's arms buildup, though intended for more immediate purposes, has had the effect of making the risk of a clash with Israel very real; it has expanded the breadth of tensions by linking conflicts and increasing insecurity generally. Lacking an urgent rationale for nuclear weapons, Iran's program has aroused Israeli fears and suspicions; they ascribe to Iran greater willingness to take military risks over broader issues than the record suggests is likely. Above all Iran's rhetoric on Palestine and its missile program raise the possibility of inviting confrontations that Iran has not considered seriously.

There is no sign that Iran's arms buildup has made the resort to force more probable because it is more available. Nothing in the record suggests that Iran has illusions about its own military power. However its experience and the lessons driving its current programs dictate the need for various types of arms: this diversified arsenal raises specters of military options that had not earlier been possible. This capability in turn raises questions for the United States, the Gulf states and Israel about Iran's intentions, the stopping point of the buildup and its implications for their security interests.

As a result of missile proliferation and the prospective diffusion of weapons of mass destruction, various zones of conflict are more intimately linked than before, enmeshing multiple axes of hostility and instability. Where intentions are unknown the combination of rhetoric and capability take on greater importance. Given the degree of damage accompanying any use of these weapons, states will tend to err on the side of caution. Thus weapons of mass destruction combined with the dangers of surprise attack could heighten pressures for preemptive or preventive war. These new classes of weapons and their implications raise crisis stability and arms control to a renewed level of importance. Iran, unconcerned with arms control, has yet to recognize that planning for security is not a unilateral enterprise; weapons with greater potential for damage and longer reach make sensitivity to the concerns of others more, not less, necessary.

DECISIONMAKING AND NATIONAL SECURITY

Revolution has marked Iran in two ways, which provide a context for and a constraint on how it makes its decisions. In contrast to Iran under the monarchy, where national security policy was formulated almost exclusively by the state, revolutionary Iran makes policy in a more untidy and altogether less consistent manner. Animated by the impulse to play an international role and motivated by ideology, Iran's decisionmaking is subject to the play of domestic political forces. These often pull in different directions providing little sense of strategic direction. They also dictate the adoption of policies that will encounter the least resistance—often as a way of forging a consensus which is elusive on domestic issues.

THE DOMESTIC CONTEXT: FOREIGN POLICY AS COMMON GROUND AMONG WARRING FACTIONS

As in most revolutions, foreign policy has played a major role in Iran's revolution. Not content with internal change revolutionaries depict their cause as a universal one, promising not to rest before they have extended the benefits of the new order to other states and assisted the liberation of other oppressed masses. Foreign policy provides a mirror for revolution, indicating its general appeal and its inherent dynamism as well as its selfless values. Foreign policy quickly becomes a central element of the revolution's legitimacy, as the regime demonstrates its vitality and commitment to its historic mission in the response it evokes among other states.

The mission's importance may take second place to the needs of the revolution itself during war and may decline with the passage of time. However, its importance may also increase if the revolutionary regime is unable to come to grips with the practical problems of governing and of securing consensus on domestic issues. This is currently the case in Iran; the revolutionary mission, and foreign policy along with it, have assumed a more central role—substituting for domestic performance; serving as a diversion from the hopeless tasks of day-to-day governance; maintaining a sense of momentum and mission; and preserving some semblance of consensus among the leadership and factions who are otherwise divided about the course the country ought to adopt.

In its foreign policy the revolution can adhere to its pristine principles, pronouncing and posturing without necessarily performing. Stances on Bosnia or Algeria are not domestically controversial, and they have the added benefit of positioning Iran in the forefront of the Islamic states, making others look selfish or miserly. In its policy toward Israel, the regime can appear to be militant without taking part directly in military engagements.

Foreign policy can also be used to deflect criticism in domestic politics. Iran's leaders can claim successes abroad, despite playing little or no actual role there: "The position of Islamic Iran and the revolution has found its appropriate status in the region and the world, to our north, [where] tens of millions of Muslims who were held captive by Marxism have been freed and several Islamic countries are merging in the new geopolitical configuration of the world.[1]

The regime can also invoke foreign policy as an excuse or reason why criticism of Iran (for instance regarding domestic failures) should be suspended: since Iran is trying hard to fight injustice abroad, achieving justice at home may take a little longer. Thus, President Rafsanjani observed that Iran was causing all sorts of problems for the United States hence it was under pressure from Washington; he asked that domestic critics take this into account.[2]

Another dimension of foreign policy's role in the revolution is as a "core value." Rhetoric and one-upmanship aside, some issues assume greater salience because others have been jettisoned. As ideological baggage is discarded, the remaining beliefs acquire more significance. Departure from those becomes all the harder because they may represent the only common ground among various factions in Iran who agree on little else. These issues, such as the stance on Israel and Palestine, are part of the original agenda of the revolution: they provide a focal point for the regime on which most elements can agree (and on which policy is verbal rather than practical). An attempt to change directions on such a policy would require a willingness to confront groups that can claim the sanction of Khomeini's legacy; to be accused of selling out the revolution; to deal with factions that will use the same kind of legitimacy issue (through foreign policy) against the leadership for their own partisan purposes. Above all, embarking on any new foreign policy requires forging a new consensus, whether by shifting the terms or by forming a dominant coalition able to pursue policies unhampered by domestic constraints. The real practical difficulty has been securing agreement on goals. Rafsanjani's query epitomizes the issue: "If the success of the revolution does not lie in its mission, then where does it lie?"[3]

The definition of that mission in the 1990s has been the object of intense political struggle since Ayatollah Khomeini's death in June 1989. Because its domestic content is the more politically salient and contentious aspect, security issues broadly defined tend to be subsumed under them. They function as a sounding board or diversion, a focus for broad consensus and a legitimator of the regime's overall policies.[4]

THE DOMESTIC CONSTRAINT: THE WAVERING APPEAL OF REVOLUTION

Support for the variously defined principles of the revolution has come increasingly into conflict with shifts in the political context within Iran itself. A key feature of the Iranian populace since 1988 has been a sense of exhaustion, saturation with revolutionary excess and an attendant loss of zeal. This fatigue is accompanied by greater interest in the state of the domestic economy. Both of these tendencies make the allocation of increasingly scarce resources to foreign affairs or foreign countries more problematic. At the same time, they limit the regime's ability to demand further sacrifices of their supporters or to mobilize them on less-than-critical issues. A changed political environment, marked by "normalization" as opposed to constant crisis, contrasts with the tendency of some members of the leadership to appeal to the revolution's early days and call for equivalent sacrifices. Yet appeal to the early principles and standards is a constant refrain and one that tends to invest ongoing policies with a validation and momentum that is hard to derail.

This fact—the difficulty of denying the revolution's original principles—interacts with another new reality—the decentralization of power—to make for many voices in foreign policy. Iran's takes dual (and opposite) approaches to many states: emphasizing good relations while undermining them (the Gulf states); dealing with governments while supporting revolutionary groups opposed to them (Turkey and the Kurdish Workers' Party); pursuing pragmatic policies then jeopardizing these openings through terrorism (as with Britain since 1989 and France since 1991). Seeking to gather the fruits of both normal ties and revolutionary practices have made for an incoherent foreign policy.

The system with several centers of power reflects not broad consensus but querulous diversity; policy results from competition and trade-offs, generating inconsistency and contradictions. If the price of getting one policy adopted is the acceptance of another group's pet scheme, the lines of various policies will diverge. With little consensus on domestic issues, Iran speaks with many voices on security issues; the erraticism of its policies is thus attributable as much to its fragmented system of power as to any Machiavellian calculation to have it both ways. Khomeini encouraged this situation and used it to enhance his own position as arbiter when he chose to intervene. Since his death, the dispersion of opinion has been aggravated, with the bonds holding the revolution together increasingly subject to centrifugal forces and no single leader of comparable stature emerging to act as arbiter of last resort.[5]

IRAN'S DECISIONMAKING: EXTREMIST NORMS/OPAQUE PROCESS

The government in Iran has no freedom in foreign policy. Khomeini's legacy, oblivious to costs and practicalities until the end of the war with Iraq, combined with the mythical dimensions of Iran's wartime sacrifice are a heavy burden; breaking free of the inertia of revolutionary commitments is difficult.

With its informal style of decisionmaking and politics and multiple centers of power—which encompass clergy and Revolutionary Guard, the extended families of senior clerics and the alliances among them—formal institutions like the Parliament (Majlis) are only a part of the constellation of authority. Iran's government is subject to an internal consensus and tied to a hard line that has been defined by its more militant anti-Western factions. Any departure from this line must be justified. In practice this creates a bias in favor of extremism; pragmatism has to be defended while generalized revolutionary activity does not. The hard-liners thus set the parameters of the internal debate, even though they rarely meaningfully consult the broader populace. Politics in Iran is less about taking the pulse than stirring up the passions.

Decisionmaking in Iran is opaque. The country is governed by consensus and by a collective responsibility among the president, cabinet and Parliament. Various bodies have a right to vet legislation for its Islamic content, and the press conducts debates on some of the issues of the day, reflecting the various political divisions. The president chooses ministers subject to approval by the Majlis; they tend increasingly to be technocrats, with little scope for initiative. Cabinet ministers are bound by a sense of what is generally acceptable, which is a product of the prevailing atmosphere and the state of play among the principal power contenders at a given time. Interest groups have inputs at all levels of decisionmaking, while technocrats are only consulted out of necessity. The continued disdain for expertise and bias toward political loyalty favors the recruitment of ideologues and slights more knowledgeable individuals. This predicament points to the important question of whether such a system based on improvisation is capable of identifying and following a strategic plan in its manifold forms or is consigned to doing no more than setting a broad strategic direction.

Little is known about how Iran makes decisions regarding national security.[6] The Supreme National Security Council has a mixed membership of clerics, senior military officers, Revolutionary Guard officers, selected diplomats and political advisors. President Rafsanjani is reported to be its active chair. (See Figure 1.) Its decisions are published but its debates are

Figure 1. IRAN'S SECURITY ORGANIZATION [a]

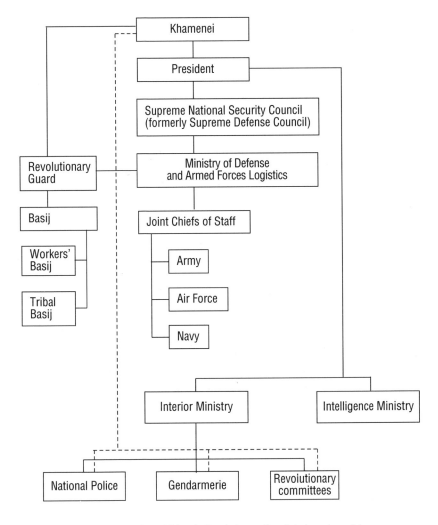

a. 1989, not without difficulty and delay, the Revolutionary Guard's independent ministry was merged with the Defense Ministry under the new Ministry of Defense and Armed Forces Logistics.

After Khomeini's death the government structure was changed. Rafsanjani, who had become chief of the armed forces in the Spring of 1988 resigned the post in September 1989, whereupon Rahbar Khamenei formally became chief of the armed forces. Rafsanjani assumed the post of a strong executive president and the position of prime minister was abolished.

The Supreme Defense Council during the Iran-Iraq War has evolved into the broader Supreme National Security Council. This should not be confused with the recently formed State Security Council (Persian: showray-e amniyat-e keshvar) chaired by the interior minister, currently Ali Mohammad Besharati-Jaromi. Since 1989, the Interior Ministry has been formally charged with control of the unified gendarmerie, police and revolutionary committees known as Nirouhay-e Entezami.

Source: Adapted from Nikola Schahgaldian, *The Iranian Military under the Islamic Republic* (Santa Monica, California: Rand Corporation, 1987) R-3473-USDP, 11.

not. Convened periodically, the council acts as a forum for discussion and adopts general positions on international subjects. Its broad composition suggests an attempt to inject expertise into its assessments, shielding them from emotive or ideological inputs. While linking military and political considerations on given issues, the council also serves as a forum for maintaining consensus. Nevertheless, factionalism and the prevalence of leaks reinforce the suspicion that its debates start and end with the ideological line laid down by the most conservative advocates, whether or not they are actually present in the council or, indeed, in the formal institutions of government. Their control of such key constituencies as the Guard, and their links to the regime's hard-core supporters—the Mustazefin (the oppressed) and the Basij—makes the clerical hard-liners disproportionately influential. Ayatollah Rahbar Khamenei, Iran's spiritual leader, has been increasingly identified with them, not least to shore up his weak clerical credentials.

The secretary of the Supreme National Security Council is a cleric, Hojjat-el-eslam Hasan Rouhani, who is also chairman of the Majlis's Foreign Affairs Committee. Rouhani and Ahmed Khomeini are present as the nominated representatives of Rahbar Khamenei. (An earlier representative was Hojjat-el-eslam Nateq Nouri, at that time minister of interior.) The assignment is normally for two years and is renewable. Most discussions in this council, which includes such figures as Ayatollah Khomeini's son, Ahmad, are necessarily general. Those attending are not present as a result of their expertise or experience. Discussions thus tend to mirror domestic positions rather than transcend them. Some formal announcements (such as the one on the Abu Musa dispute) appear to be intended for a domestic rather than for an international audience. The council tends to adopt lowest common denominator positions that associate all groups with policy decisions. It thus accepts rather than rises above internal divisions. Where the decision to be taken is controversial, as was the acceptance of the cease-fire in the war with Iraq, the council provides a vehicle for associating all factions with it.

Decisionmaking regarding the armed forces is no more penetrable. The Revolutionary Guard (Pasdaran) is the favored force of the clerical leadership. It has its own sponsors, a domestic constituency and such allies as the powerful, para-statal Martyr's Foundation. It also has preferences and networks of its own in foreign affairs, notably in cooperating with Syria, Pakistan, China and North Korea. The Guard's involvement extends to Lebanon and the Sudan and it has been responsible for training (religious) opposition forces in other countries (such as Turkey). The

Guard has a subunit dedicated to the export of the revolution that appears to be involved in covert activities with the security services. How independent or autonomous the Pasdaran is in relations with the civilian leadership depends on the issue. (See Figure 2.) Where large expenditures of foreign exchange are concerned, it is probably subject to control. But in revolutionary activities abroad, it is in a position to play on differences among the leadership to pursue its own agenda. The regular forces, especially the professional cadres, are certainly subject to greater political oversight, both internally through clerical commissars and institutionally. Their opinion is paid greater heed when technical input is needed, and they are respected for their expertise but distrusted politically.

The Atomic Energy Organization, comprised of nuclear specialists, energy experts, scientists, engineers and others, debates issues concerning the nuclear program. Procurement of technology and materials appears to be direct and indirect, through the organization and through universities and research centers. The organization is headed by Dr. Reza Amrollahi, a technician, who holds the governmental rank of vice-president, which suggests the importance attached to the program. Other principal actors include Rafsanjani and Mohsen Rezai, the head of the Guard. (The security of the Atomic Energy Organization's facilities and laboratories is under the Guard.) There are few signs of any debate about the purposes of the nuclear program, which is characterized publicly as a question of access to modern science. If the budget were significant or growing, such a debate would be unavoidable.

What conclusions can be derived from this summary of the forces bearing on decisionmaking?

- The regime is fraught with political divisions and lacks a consensus on any but the basic issue of retaining power. On fundamental issues of regime survival (the cease-fire) the principals hang together. On others, differences persist. This is aggravated by the decentralization of power, making the implementation of a single coherent policy impossible.

- Forging a new consensus or changing policy is difficult; the force of inertia is strong. Hard-liners set the terms of the debate: they take a "show me" attitude toward change, shifting the burden of proof to any party proposing change.[7]

- Political rifts and domestic jockeying for power bar the formulation of

Figure 2. THE REVOLUTIONARY GUARD'S INTERNAL STRUCTURE [a]

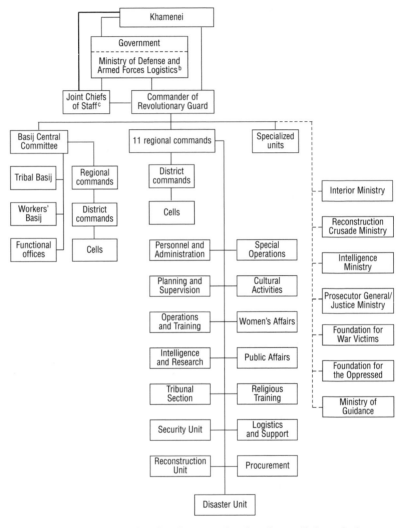

a. The Revolutionary Guard has been formally integrated to a large degree with the regular forces. However, its basic responsibilities, which now focus on internal security, remain variegated. Indicative of the scope of the organization and operations is this chart based on information from 1987. Despite the formal abolition of the Guard Ministry, most of the activities indicated continue. There is continued direct access to Rahbar Khamenei.

b. The former Minister of Armed Force Logistics and Defense Akbar Torkan was replaced in the Fall of 1993 by Mohammad Foruzandeh.

c. The Office of the Joint Chiefs of Staff, created in 1988, in theory combines the regular forces and the Revolutionary Guard. The current holder, Hassan Firouzabadi, a civilian, oversees the Supreme Council for military policy which is responsible for the clarification of missions and integration of the command structure of the armed forces.

Source: Chart adapted from Schahgaldian, *The Iranian Military*, 77. Text by author.

long-term policies. From the record it appears extremely doubtful that Iran is capable of pursuing a long-term integrated strategy. The perspective, the requisite assurance of political power and the organizational capacity simply do not exist. In the war with Iraq, Tehran demonstrated an inability to integrate resources and goals; it excelled in tactical and short-term expedients.[8] Conditions since Khomeini's demise have deteriorated, both politically and in terms of availability of resources. To pursue a nuclear weapons program successfully would require an internal consensus on allocation of resources, the conviction that it would pay off in a limited time, agreement on who would control it and a long-term view that assumed the political longevity of the decisionmakers. (None of these are present in a regime such as Iran's; by contrast, Iraq, with one leader, meets all of these conditions.)

- Foreign policy is a device for legitimating the regime. Since domestic performance has been deficient, foreign policy has come to serve as a substitute. Hard-line positions (on Israel and Palestine for instance) reflect ideological and tactical considerations. Abrupt policy shifts are not ruled out, however—if the price of the old one is too high or if the attractions of changing policy increase.[9]

- Although Iran's policies can be said to have a "strategic direction" (seeking to increase Iran's influence and power and weaken its enemies, notably the United States and its "clients") there is no strategic program, no timetable or deadlines, and no analysis of costs, trade-offs or alternatives. Iran's policies evolve and, given domestic policies, take on lives of their own. Its policies toward Israel and Syria are examples of this. Despite the evidence that a Syrian-Israeli agreement is more likely than ever before, Iran has hardened its stance, giving itself less room to maneuver with little consideration as to its own options.

- Since there is no hand at the helm, and little institutional influence (Foreign Ministry input or the like), there is no learning process. Feedback is not used to adjust course. As a result changes in direction tend to be abrupt rather than incremental, the product of force rather than adaptation. Since decisionmaking tends to be reactive rather than anticipatory, policy lurches from crisis to crisis. Rather than delineating a clear pattern of priorities and goals, decisions are the product of an internal struggle for power in which competing visions of the future of Iran are but one element in the stakes.

CONCLUSIONS

Iran's experience as a revolutionary state has reinforced its sense of embattlement. Its war with Iraq and the allies' military response to Iraq's aggression against Kuwait have instilled in Iran a healthy respect for military power. The general lessons derived from these events, such as preparedness and self-reliance, are unexceptional. However Iran's sense of grievance, fueled by international apathy at Iraq's use of chemical weapons and missiles against it, now drives it to acquire the same capability as retaliatory weapons to avoid future surprises. Its embryonic nuclear program appears to be designed as a general hedge, an option, rather than a crash program with a particular enemy in mind.

Iran's defense policies are as much the product of the war and its experience as of strategic calculation. The shift to Russian, North Korean and Chinese arms was unavoidable when Western sources of supply dried up. The search for missiles was dictated as much by the lack of spare parts for its (U.S.-supplied) air force as by preference. Missiles perforce became the weapon of choice for Iran when the task of keeping its air force operational became problematic. As substitutes missiles were not perfect, but they did reduce reliance on suppliers and helped the revolutionaries in severing the umbilical cord of dependency. As an added bonus, missiles reduced the regime's dependence on the professional military, an institution the clerics distrusted as prototypically modern. Finally, missiles became attractive as retaliatory weapons with assured penetration.

There is no clear relationship between Iran's threat perception, force structure, missions, doctrine, and procurement policy on the one hand and what it can afford on the other. Iran's scramble to buy whatever arms are available today is a response to a decade of near-total embargo and a sense that it might be reimposed again at any time. That its military programs lack a strategic blueprint and may not be the result of an integrated effort is no comfort to its neighbors, however.

Iran's military establishment thus mirrors its recent experience and its current opportunities. Its arms programs testify to the importance its leaders attach to military power, especially as the costs of these programs compete with pressing economic and social needs. Whether or not Iran's inventory today matches that of the past, its neighbors see current investments as indicative of its current priorities. The smaller Arab states are not disposed to be sensitive to claims that Iran was the victim of Iraqi aggression or that the purpose behind its buildup is defensive. So whatever its intentions, Iran's buildup increases regional tensions.

Iran's conventional arms program command more attention than its operational capacities warrant. Lacking power projection capability, their effective area of activity is limited. Iran's airpower is circumscribed by the difficulties of maintaining aircraft of two different origins and eventually of shifting to another source entirely (one, moreover, with a poor record of service and support). Any inclination to coerce its neighbors will be conditioned as much by political realities as by their own military capabilities. Iran's dependence on oil and on harmonious working relations with its OPEC partners dictates good behavior. Moreover, as long as the United States maintains a concrete commitment in the vicinity, Iran will be deterred from risking confrontation.

Nonconventional weapons are unlikely to be used short of all-out war. With the possible exception of Iraq, Iran has no particular claim or cause to engage in such a war. The shadow of these weapons nevertheless has its own effect. A regional arms race in missiles, theater anti-ballistic missiles and aircraft is one distinct possibility. Requests for security guarantees against nuclear blackmail by the smaller Gulf states may arise as and if the nuclearization of the region spreads. The need for regional arms control and more comprehensive arms control will increase with the spread of longer-range weapons. At that juncture, the exclusion of one or more states from such agreements would tend to undermine them.

Iran at present is no more than a nuisance militarily although it could become a more serious threat over the next decade. Externally, three variables could change the picture. The destabilization of Saudi Arabia due to domestic unrest and political strife would increase Iran's importance. A major rift between China and the West might permit the emergence of an alliance between China and Iran that would improve Iran's ability to pursue its present course. Finally, shifts in Russia's foreign policy that emphasized assertiveness toward the West and domination of its frontiers might bring Iran into play as a potential Russian partner. None of these developments is imminent, all are possible, and any one of them would increase Iran's room for maneuver.

The success of the revolution and the future of the Islamic Republic of Iran will be determined by its economic performance. This stark reality is palpably obvious to most Iranians despite its vehement denial by leaders who seek diversions, rhetorical pyrotechnics and excuses. The revolution today is a hollow shell that neither inspires nor animates its proponents. The costs of the war, economic mismanagement, corruption, rapid population growth (averaging 3.5 percent annually) and the slide in the value of oil have combined to devastate the Iranian economy. By every indicator Iran is worse off economically than in the Shah's reign.[1] The costs of reconstruction include renewing a neglected infrastructure, a task complicated now by the pressure of growth and the drift of the population into the cities.[2] Keeping this young populace clothed, fed and schooled, and providing it with medical attention and employment opportunities constitutes the most difficult and urgent task for any government in Tehran. As a country that has experienced prosperity in living memory, economic issues are of special political salience.

Economic needs will inevitably influence resource allocations and political priorities. They may affect security negatively in at least two ways. Economic deterioration may feed disintegrative tendencies. As the center is unable to provide resources and services, outlying regions may reconsider the benefits of national unity. Drawn by such tendencies, Iranian Azerbaijan and Iranian Kurdistan may be candidates for secession. A second scenario is one in which economic desperation, along Saddam Hussein's model, leads to a resource grab—an act of aggression against a small vulnerable neighbor.

Unless Iran improves its economic performance it will face the prospect of civil disturbance, as occurred twice in 1992 and again more recently. Increasingly it may have to rely on coercion to secure domestic order. With its sense of mission, ambition for status and opportunistic attitude toward regional developments, Iran's military programs have caused great disquiet. This would multiply if the regime were to become domestically more volatile as well. Iran's daunting economic problems will constrain many programs; orders will go unsigned or deliveries will fail to materialize; projects, including ambitious nuclear programs, will be stretched out, refinanced or cut. Iran will become more sensitive to costs in coming years. Iran's reconstruction is hampered today by the country's inability to expand its short- and long-term credits and increase its oil and gas revenues. Neither is likely without improved relations with the West.

Current Iranian politics do not reflect this narrowing horizon. The regime's hard-liners argue that Rafsanjani's attempts at pragmatism have yielded no benefits, either in funds from the West or goodwill from Iran's neighbors. They have therefore redoubled their efforts at extremism, rejecting the Palestinian-Israeli agreement and hurling imprecations at states accepting the "sell-out." Domestically, Islamic standards have been reimposed, the usual suspects rounded up and the United States anathematized. This hard line, a policy dead-end, has few supporters and little life left in it. Inevitably the cost of such policies will be felt and will ultimately force changes in policy.

Iran is adamant that certain preconditions (such as release of disputed "assets") be met before discussions with the United States are possible.

Voices inside Iran are heard arguing for a resumption of relations with the United States as a means of improving dialogue, if only to clarify the true areas of disagreement. The divided leadership resists this, fearing a loss of control if the faintest whiff of discussions about normalization were to gain currency. The reality in Iran today (as elsewhere) is deep ambivalence: receptivity to U.S. culture, a thirst for contact and a determination to go their own way. Satellite television and videos make interaction inevitable and impervious to control. The leadership in Iran speaks of cultural "threats," cultural "bullets" and the need to maintain cultural "authenticity." This will not be easy short of isolation. Yet the trend toward interdependence in virtually all areas is well-nigh irresistible.

Iranian leaders have depicted the United States as an all-purpose bogy, exploiting the paranoid strain prevalent in their domestic politics.[3] This has provided them with time, which they have squandered. Intransigence and confrontational rhetoric have become substitutes for policies to deal with increasing national disenchantment with the Islamic Republic. International status will not substitute for domestic performance; in fact Iran will have no status whatsoever without it. Iran's attempt to rectify the ills of its own society has taken the form of blaming others and seeking vicarious satisfaction abroad. This has aggravated those problems that lend themselves neither to crash programs nor ideological solutions. Iran's national security has been threatened as much by its overweening ambitions and excesses as by aggressive neighbors. A more modest approach would go far toward satisfying its basic needs, at lesser cost.

Table 7.   PROBABLE POSITIONS OF DIFFERENT IRANIAN REGIMES ON SPECIFIC ISSUES IN FOREIGN AFFAIRS

	Shah[a]	National[b]	IRI[c]
Would it seek regional influence in the Gulf?	yes	yes	yes
Would it seek regional influence in the Caucasus and Central Asia?	yes	yes	yes
Would it seek regional influence in Afghanistan?	yes	yes	yes
Would it pursue a pattern of hostility toward the U.S.?	no	unknown/ no	no
Would it engage in a military buildup?	yes	yes	yes
Would it seek to acquire chemical or nuclear weapons?	unknown/ no	unknown/ no	yes
Would it support or sponsor terrorism?[d]	no	no	yes
Would it oppose Israel?	no	no	yes
Would it be involved in Sudan and Algeria?	no	no	yes
Would it be in competition with Turkey?	no	unknown	yes
Would it have problems with the Kurds?	no	unknown	yes

a. Monarchical predecessor to current regime.
b. Putative secular-nationalist alternative government.
c. Islamic Republic of Iran.
d. Note where the IRI's position stands out: on terrorism, Israel, wider involvement in Islamic issues (for instance Sudan, Algeria), and nuclear and chemical weapons.

END NOTES

The following sources and terms are abbreviated in the notes:

BBC Summary of World Broadcasts for the Middle East: ME/...

BBC Summary of World Broadcasts for the Soviet Union: SU/...

Federal Broadcast Information Service: FBIS-...

Voice of the Islamic Republic of Iran (radio broadcast): *Voice of the IRI*

Vision of the Islamic Republic of Iran (television broadcast): *Vision of the IRI*

Islamic Republic News Agency: IRNA

IRAN'S SECURITY PERSPECTIVES: LOCAL, REGIONAL AND INTERNATIONAL

[1] In Azerbaijan the threat to Iran could be multiple: Northern Azerbaijan could politicize Iranian Azerbaijan, increase demands among the latter for secession, or increase pressures or demands for Iranian involvement in the war against Armenia. Iranian minorities would not be directly affected by internal fissures in Tajikistan and Afghanistan, but linguistic and sectarian ties would create demands for some response. At best, these scenarios pose the threat of instability on borders, at worst the disintegration of states with possible spillover: Iran is thus faced with immediate problems.

[2] Since mid-August 1992 U.S. forces in the Persian Gulf region have stood at 24,000 (versus 10,000 in August 1990). In addition to some seventy land-based aircraft in Saudi Arabia, there are seventy aircraft in a ten-ship battle group deployed in the northern Gulf. See Dore Gold, "The U.S. and Gulf Security," in Shlomo Gazit and others, The Middle East Military Balance 1992-93 (Tel Aviv: Jerusalem Post Press, Jaffee Center for Strategic Studies, 1993) p. 84.

[3] See Barton Gellman, "Temper Tantrums of a Gulf War Hero," *International Herald Tribune*, July 26, 1993.

[4] Exclusion zones in northern and southern Iraq limit Iraq's ability to enter with its armed forces at will, especially by air.

[5] An Iranian newspaper characterized the U.S. action of shadowing a Chi-

nese freighter suspected of carrying chemical weapons precursors to Iran as piracy; at the very least the act conformed with the prevailing view of the United States as bully. See report of the daily *Jomhuri-ye Islami* carried on the radio broadcast, *Voice of the Islamic Republic of Iran (IRI)*, Tehran, August 12 in BBC Summary of World Broadcasts/ME/1767/A/11 (hereinafter cited as "ME/...") August 14, 1993.

[6] See the comments of Islam Karimov, the Uzbek president, in *Nezavisimaya Gazeta Moscow*, September 17 in BBC Summary of World Broadcasts/SU/1490/A12-3 (hereinafter cited as "SU/..."), September 19, 1992. He repeated them in an interview on Mayak radio, Moscow (September 28 in SU/1499/B/17-18, September 30, 1992) but here the evidence, if anything, is of Iran's reluctance. As Iranian President Hashemi Rafsanjani put it, Iran was "unhappy" about the course of the civil war, not to mention Russian and Uzbek interference, but stated that "unfortunately...our hands are not long enough to extend in all directions to solve all problems." Rafsanjani, Friday sermon at Khomeini's shrine (February 5 in ME/1607/A/8 February 8, 1993). For an excellent discussion of Russia's foreign policy tendencies in this area see, Mohiaddin Mesbahi, "Russian Foreign Policy and Security in Central Asia and the Caucasus," *Central Asian Survey* 12, no. 2 (July 1993): 181-215.

[7] See Serge Schmemann, "Turkey Holds Talks on Caucasus War," *New York Times*, September 10, 1993, p. A3; Margaret Shapiro, "Russian Mediation Urged in Caucasus," *Washington Post*, September 9, 1993.

[8] See the interview with Nateq Nouri, speaker of the Iranian Majlis (parliament), in *Middle East Insight* 10, no. 5 (July-August 1993): 26. For greater detail see Shahram Chubin, "Postwar Gulf Security," *Survival* 32, no. 2 (March-April 1991): 140-57, and Shahram Chubin, "Iran and Collective Security in the Gulf," *Survival* 34, no. 3 (Autumn 1992): 62-80.

[9] For example the Abu Musa episode, which the Arab Gulf states saw as a case of muscle-flexing by Iran and an attempt to annex an island whose sovereignty, though disputed, was shared with Sharjah, one of the United Arab Emirates.

[10] The price of oil in 1993 was approximately $15 a barrel. See Youssef Ibrahim "Oil Prices Plunging, May Not Have Hit Bottom," *New York Times*, September 13, 1993, p. D1.

[11] See Charles Tripp and Shahram Chubin, "Domestic Politics and Territorial Disputes in the Persian Gulf and Arabian Peninsula," *Survival* 35, no. 4 (Winter 1993-94) 3-27.

[12] Iranian passivity or restraint was notable in spring 1991 when a Shi'i uprising took place in southern Iraq while Saddam's regime was in disarray. Iran has not been overly active even after southern Iraq became somewhat detached as a result of the allies' "no-fly zone." In mid-1992 Iran was alleged to have some 4,000 Revolutionary Guard troops in the area, probably a reaction to Saddam's various offensives against the Shi'ites of the southern marshlands. See Tony Walker and Roger Matthews, "Arabs Divided over the Worth of No-Fly Zone in Iraq," *The Financial Times*, August 25, 1992.

[13] Bernard Lewis has suggested that the revolutionary "Islamic Republic of Iran" is more revolutionary than Islamic or Iranian. See "The Enemies of God," *The New York Review of Books*, March 25, 1993, p. 30.

[14] Nateq Nouri interview, *Middle East Insight* 27.

[15] As Hashemi Rafsanjani, president of the Islamic Republic of Iran put it, "Iran's leaders, government and people are not prepared to compromise over their revolutionary and principled positions," press conference (January 31 in ME/1602/A/2, February 2, 1993).

[16] Ayatollah Rahbar Khamenei, Iran's spiritual leader, Friday sermon (October 20 in ME/0594/A/1, October 23, 1989). Elsewhere Khamenei insists that it is Iran's fight against oppression that "has turned the Islamic Republic into a role model for which the world has respect," Air Force Day address (January 8 in ME/1609/A/4, February 10, 1993).

[17] Khamenei, *Voice of the IRI* (November 26 in ME/0626/A/8, November 29, 1989).

[18] Khamenei, *Voice of the IRI* (June 3 in ME/1399/A/1, June 5, 1992).

[19] Khamenei, *Voice of the IRI* (February 9 in ME/0686/A/1, February 12, 1990). He voiced a more militant version of this idea in September 1989: "Defending Islam will not merely be confined to defending the Islamic homeland. We are prepared to fight and wage jihad against blasphemy on

all frontiers of Islam," BBC, September 29, 1989. This has not been re-peated.

[20] See "Cross Frontier Broadcasting," *The Economist*, May 2, 1992, pp. 21-28. Iran also has an Islamic propagation organization supporting missionaries, writers and publications in more than twenty countries. See the report of the television broadcast, *Vision of the Islamic Republic of Iran (IRI)* (June 22 in ME/1416/A/3-5, June 25, 1992).

[21] Nelson Mandela, the African National Congress's President told his Iranian hosts in July 1992: "The people of Africa will make Iran's Islamic revolution a model for their revolutionary moves," *The Economist*, July 25, 1992, p. 44.

[22] Khamenei consistently refers to it as "the main problem of the Islamic world." Rafsanjani has summarized the issue as follows: "The Palestine question is an Islamic one and we have a say in it. We are involved. It is our right to demand [that] an injustice has been committed and has to be corrected." Press conference (January 31 in ME/1604/A/12, February 4, 1993).

[23] U.S. statements lend credence to this. Former Secretary of State James Baker, for one, claims that the United States's victories in the cold war and in Desert Storm created the conditions that have made negotiations possible and success likely. See Elaine Sciolino, "As History Unfolds, U.S. Takes to Sidelines," *New York Times*, September 9, 1993, p. A12.

[24] This figure is an approximation based on the $60 million annually given to Hezbollah in the past and an estimate of the smaller amount (which given conditions in Gaza goes further) dispersed to Hamas and Islamic Jihad. The numbers represent best guesses from a number of sources, including Israeli. For one published source see, Bhatia Shyam, "Iran Backs Bid of Islamic Zealots to Undermine Arafat and PLO," *The Observer* (London), November 1, 1992.

[25] See "Khomenei's Son Denounces Mid-East Accord, Calling it Treachery," *New York Times*, September 13, 1993, and "Iranian President Denounces Accord," *Washington Post*, September 15, 1993, p. A26.

[26] Lebanon's Shi'i comprise 32 percent of the population. For this and

other figures relating to Shi'i populations in the Islamic world see Martin Kramer, ed., *Shi'ism, Resistance and Revolution*, Boulder, Colo./London: Westview/Mansell, 1987, 10.

[27] The conference called on Islamic countries to establish permanent military units assigned to a Jerusalem liberation army. Conference participants asked Iran to set up a secretariat to implement this and other resolutions. One resolution affirmed the "undeniable sovereignty of the Palestinian people over the entire Palestinian territory" and called for "the elimination of Zionist existence." See "Officials Comment on Tehran Conference on Palestine," *Vision of the IRI* (October 22 in FBIS-NES-91-205, October 23, 1991, p. 9). For an Israeli reaction see Defense Minister Moshe Arens, *Voice of Israel* (October 30 in ME/1218/A/3-4, November 1, 1991). President Rafsanjani has referred to Israel as an "illegitimate" state and said that it "must be isolated by all countries." Iran, he declared, "would give any form of help possible to the people of Palestine for the realization of [their] rights." Press conference (January 31 in ME/1604/A/10, February 4, 1993).

[28] The Taif Agreement is a 1989 national charter to end civil strife in Lebanon. It was negotiated in Taif, Saudi Arabia, by Lebanese Muslim and Christian leaders.

[29] Foreign Ministry statement reported by the *Voice of the IRI* (August 8 in ME/1762/A/7, August 9, 1993).

THE LESSONS OF IRAN'S RECENT EXPERIENCE

[1] See, in particular Shahram Chubin "The Conduct of Military Operations," *Politique Etrangere*, special issue: "Iran-Irak La Diplomatie du Conflit," no. 2 (1987): 303-16: Shahram Chubin, "From Stalemate to Ceasefire: Iran and the War," in Efraim Karsh, ed., *The Iran-Iraq War: Impact and Implications* (London: Macmillan, 1989) 13-25.

[2] See citation in Chubin, "From Stalemate to Ceasefire," 15. For a comprehensive source listing and an elaboration of the lessons derived from the Gulf wars see Shahram Chubin, "Iran and the Lessons of the War with Iraq," in Shelley Stahl and Geoffrey Kemp, eds., *Arms Control and Weapons Proliferation in the Middle East and South Asia* (New York: St. Martin's Press [in association with the Carnegie Endowment for Interna-

tional Peace], 1992). See also Shahram Chubin, "Iran: The Lessons of Desert Storm" unpublished paper prepared for Los Alamos National Laboratory, November 1991.

[3] *Voice of the IRI* (October 20 and in ME/0594/A/3, October 23, 1989).

[4] For representative comments from Rafsanjani, Khamenei and Ayatollah Montazeri (at that time Khomeini's designated successor) see IRNA (Islamic Republic News Agency) Tehran home service (February 8 in ME/0381/A/1-4, February 10, 1989); *Tehran Times* (February 13) and IRNA (February 13) in ME/0384/A/5-6, February 14, 1989.

[5] Tehran TV (September 22 in ME/0267/A/3, September 27, 1988); Tehran home service (September 18 in ME/0264/A/1-5, September 23, 1988).

[6] Tehran home service (October 6 in ME/0277/A/4, October 8, 1988).

[7] "We will try to get weapons from a variety of sources," Deputy Foreign Minister Ahmed Besharati stated in an interview with *Voice of the IRI* (November 21 in ME/0621/A/1, November 23, 1989). Rafsanjani has suggested that relative self-sufficiency is a strategic aim: "We must have a strong base for our own needs so that we are not open to blackmail," *Voice of the IRI* (July 25 in ME/1443/A/8-9, July 27, 1992).

[8] Naser Heyrani-Nobari, Iran's ambassador to the USSR, IRNA in English (February 27 in ME/0701/A/5, March 1, 1990).

[9] For an overview of Iran's arms industries, see Anoushirivan Ehteshami, "Iran's Revolution: Fewer Ploughshares, More Swords," *Army Quarterly and Defence Journal* 120, no. 1 (January 1990): 41-50. For an earlier discussion see Ann Schulz, "Iran: An Enclave Arms Industry," *1986 SIPRI Yearbook: World Armament and Disarmament*, (London: Oxford University Press, 1987) 147-61.

[10] See the discussion on the "Political Roundtable," Tehran TV, (April 7 in ME/0122/A/5-9, April 11, 1988) and John H. Cushman, Jr., "Iran Says It Is Expanding Its Ability to Make Arms," New York Times, September 13, 1987.

[11] Roger Matthews, "Maintaining Iran's Integrity," interview with Iran's minister for defense logistics, Akbar Torkan, *The Financial Times* (survey on Iran), February 8, 1993.

[12] Khamenei (IRNA, July 30 in ME/1756/A/15, August 2, 1993).

[13] Chubin, "Lessons of Desert Storm."

[14] See *The Independent*, March 22, 1988, and *The Washington Post*, March 10, 1988. See also Steve Zaloga, "Ballistic Missiles in the Third World," *International Defense Review*, no. 11 (1988): 1,427; and W. Seth Carus and Joseph S. Bermudez, "Iran's Emerging Missile Forces," *Jane's Defence Weekly*, July 23, 1988, pp. 126-31.

[15] *International Herald Tribune*, July 20, 1987; see Rafsanjani's speech in Qom (September 24 in ME/0267/A/4, September 27, 1988).

[16] See respectively, Iraq News Agency, Baghdad (July 30 in ME/0218/A/7, August 1, 1988) and Hazim Mushtak, "An Iraqi View," in Stahl and Kemp, *Arms Control and Weapons Proliferation*, especially p. 115.

[17] See Joseph Alpher, ed., *War in the Gulf: Implications for Israel* (Tel Aviv: Jerusalem Post Press, Jaffee Center for Strategic Studies, 1992) 177, et passim.

[18] See especially Rafsanjani, Tehran (June 10 in FBIS-V, III, June 12, 1984); Rafsanjani (July 31 in ME/8325/A/6, August 2, 1986).

[19] Tehran home service (March 29 in ME/0144/A/1, March 31, 1988). Rafsanjani commented, "Any time they [Iraqis] are not afraid and have not tasted their own poison, then they start mischief" Interview, Tehran home service (April 4 in ME/0118/A/3, April 6, 1988).

[20] Tehran home service (September 23 in ME/0266/A/8, September 26, 1988). [Emphasis supplied]

[21] Rafsanjani, Tehran home service (October 18 in ME/0278/A/1, October 20, 1988).

[22] "Preparing for Protection of Our National Interests," *Resalat*

(editorial) (December 31, 1990 in FBIS-NES-91-010, January 15, 1991, p. 66); and "A Military Lesson from the Persian Gulf War," *Kayhan International*, commentary, March 17, 1991 (and March 17 in FBIS-NES-91-052, March 18, 1991, p. 81).

[23] Rafsanjani interview on Tehran TV (April 18, in ME/0130/A/6, April 20, 1988); Rafsanjani, Tehran home service (April 15 in ME/0128/A/4, April 18, 1988). The USSR was reported to have brokered a truce in the earlier air and missile exchanges in 1987. Moscow reportedly threatened that unless Tehran suspended its ground offensives in exchange for Baghdad calling a halt to its air attacks, Moscow would supply Baghdad with SS-12 missiles with a 324-mile range (540 kilometers). See *The Times* (London) February 28, 1987, and *International Herald Tribune*, February 28, 1987, and March 1, 1987.

[24] IRNA in English (April 17 in ME/0438/A/3, April 19, 1989).

[25] Roger Matthews, Akbar Torkan interview, *The Financial Times*.

[26] Shai Feldman, "Proliferation of Ballistic Missiles: Policy Options for the Future," Proceedings of an Annual Meeting Symposium (Washington, D.C.: American Association for the Advancement of Science, Program on Science, Arms Control and National Security, February 1990) 11.

[27] British experts argue that Iraq's effective use of chemical arms developed tremendously over the course of the war, raising questions about traditional notions of their limited effectiveness. Author's interviews, London, February-March 1989. See also Anthony Cordesman, *Weapons of Mass Destruction in the Middle East* (London/Washington: Brassey's, 1991) 88-92.

[28] For example, Khamenei stated, "The world tries to observe rules in war. Chemical attacks are against the rules of war," Tehran home service (April 8, 1988 in BBC). Regarding self-defense, Rafsanjani, for example, told a newspaper that Iran could equip its forces with chemical weapons but hoped it would not have to do so; interview in *La Stampa* (Rome) (April 24, IRNA, ME/0135/A/7, April 26, 1988); Rafsanjani told an international conference after the war that Iran had possessed the capability to use chemical arms during the war but had not done so out of principle (Tehran, August 11 in ME/0229/A/4, August 13, 1988). The Revolution-

ary Guard minister, Mohsen Rafikdoust, stated, "This time if chemical weapons are deployed against us, we will not hesitate to teach the enemy a lesson," (televised news conference, January 14 in ME/0050/i, January 16, 1988). Iran also threatened in the United Nations to resort to "preventive measures" if such weapons were used again. See "Le Guerre du Golfe," *Le Monde*, January 9, 1987, 5.

[29] Cordesman, *Weapons of Mass Destruction*, 90-93. W. Andrew Terrill, Jr., "Chemical Weapons in the Gulf War," *Strategic Review* 14, no. 2 (Spring 1986): 51-58; Patrick Tyler, "Iran Faulted, Too, in Gas Attack on the Kurds," *International Herald Tribune*, May 4, 1990.

[30] Akbar Velayati, Iran's foreign minister, speech to the Paris conference on chemical weapons, IRNA in English (January 7 in ME/0353/A/9, January 9, 1989).

[31] For a clear expression see Chief Justice Musavi Ardebili's comments, IRNA in English (July 25 in ME/0214/A/1, July 27, 1988).

[32] In its formal acceptance of the cease-fire in July 1988 the Iranian General Command Headquarters referred to "the extensive and unprecedented use of chemical weapons, especially in recent operations" by Iraq, noting that the global silence on the issue was an indication of a "dangerous international conspiracy," Tehran home service (July 18 in ME/0207/A/9, July 19, 1988).

[33] See Khamenei, Tehran home service (August 8, 1988, and Tehran, August 11 in ME/0229/A/4, August 13, 1988).

[34] Tehran, September 23 in ME/0226/A/8-9, September 26, 1988; Tehran, October 6 in ME/0277/A/4, October 8, 1988.

[35] Tehran home service, August 27 in ME/8659/A/4, August 29, 1987.

[36] In comments made to an international academic conference on the Persian Gulf, August 10, 1988. Tehran home service (August 11 in ME/0229/A/4, August 13, 1988).

[37] For a discussion, see the chapter by Philip Sabine in chapter 17, "Escalation and the Iran-Iraq War," 280-95, in Karsh, ed., *The Iran-Iraq War*.

[38] Rafsanjani, IRNA in English (October 19 in ME/0288/A/2, October 21, 1988).

[39] Khamenei to the U.N. Conference on Disarmament, Tehran home service (September 16 in ME/0260/A/3-4, September 19, 1988); Rafsanjani, Tehran home service (May 26 in ME/0648/A/7-8, May 29, 1989).

ARMS POLICIES AND PROGRAMS

[1] Cordesman, *Weapons of Mass Destruction*, 16, 82. Iran "only spent about one third as much as Iraq on conventional arms since the ceasefire and has not yet received any major stocks of armor or modern combat aircraft," (108). Earlier Cordesman and Wagner estimated that Iran would require "time and at least $15 to $25 billion worth of investment to recover its past military power," Anthony Cordesman and Abraham Wagner, *The Lessons of Modern War*, vol. 2, The Iran-Iraq War (Boulder, Colo./London:Westview/Mansell, 1990) 596.

[2] See *inter alia* Anthony Cordesman, "Current Trends in Arms Sales and Proliferation in the Middle East," (Washington, D.C.: Office of Senator John McCain, January 1992), 77-78.

[3] Iran increased the defense budget by less than 4 percent of GDP annually during the war according to Tehran Radio's account of an International Monetary Fund consultant mission's report. IRNA in English (September 26, in FBIS-NES-90-189, September 28, 1990, pp. 65-66).

[4] Friday sermon, *Voice of the IRI*, (May 24 in ME/1082/A/4-5, May 27, 1991).

[5] Shahram Chubin and Charles Tripp, *Iran and Iraq at War* (Boulder, Colo/London: Tauris/Westview, 1988). Nikola Schahgaldian, *The Iranian Military under the Islamic Republic* (Santa Monica, Calif.: Rand Corporation, 1987) R-3473-USDP.

[6] For a comment by Khamenei on these "differentiated responsibilities" see *Voice of the IRI*, (September 18 in ME/1182/A/8, September 20, 1991).

[7] This is the view of Kenneth Katzman, *Warriors of Islam* (Boulder, Colo.: Westview Press, 1993).

[8] The decision to integrate the Revolutionary Guard and the regular military has been carried out formally in that their command structures are coordinated at the topmost level, that is in the Joint Chiefs of Staff. These senior military officers and Pasdaran officers work in parallel and report to the senior civilian policymaker, Spiritual Leader Khamenei. The defense minister, until recently Akbar Torkan, is a civilian chosen by President Rafsanjani as part of his cabinet. The defense minister is a technocrat essentially responsible for procurement and logistics for both forces. Judging from the Guard's own foreign relations activities there is some question as to the extent of its accountability and its degree of influence regarding weapons procurement intended for its use.

[9] Richard Grimmett, *Conventional Arms Transfers to the Third World 1985-1992*, Congressional Research Service report for Congress (Washington, D.C.: Congressional Research Service, July 1993), 30-32.

[10] China has not joined the Missile Technology Control Regime (MTCR) but has agreed to honor its provisions. It limits sales of technology for missiles in excess of 500 kilograms (1,100 pounds) and a 300-kilometer (180-mile) range. China is suspected of breaking this pledge. China has an economic reason to continue arms sales. Since there is little demand for its aircraft, it sees little reason to turn away a potential customer for its missiles. At the same time its economic development has raised its oil consumption, which may require increased imports from the Persian Gulf. This would cement the economic rationale for continued exports of arms and missiles.

[11] *Arms Transfers to the Third World 1985-1992* (July 1993) 58.

[12] Figures in this and the next paragraph are drawn from *The Military Balance 1980-81* and annually through 1992-3 (London: Institute for International Strategic Studies, 1980 through 1993).

[13] Figures taken from *The Military Balance* for the years 1979 to 1992.

[14] Saudi Arabia has outspent Iran on defense by 50 to 300 percent. See especially *The Military Balance, 1985-86*, 170-71; and *The Military Balance, 1991-92*, 212-13. For arms imports see Grimmett, *Arms Transfers to the Third World 1985-1992*, 34, 58.

[15] See *The Military Balance, 1980-81*, 42-43; and Cordesman and Wagner, *Lessons of Modern War*, vol. 2, (table 3.5) 57-58.

[16] In artillery pieces, armored vehicles and helicopters for instance. See *1986 SIPRI Yearbook: World Armament and Disarmament*, 304. Compare Cordesman and Wagner, *Lessons of Modern War*, vol. 2, 429.

[17] Some sources put the figures higher, with Iraqi imports triple those of Iran over the period 1979-83 ($17.6 billion as opposed to $5.36 billion) and nearly quadruple for 1980-88 ($25 billion versus $7 billion). See respectively Cordesman and Wagner *Lessons of Modern War*, 3, 165, and Richard Grimmett, *Arms Transfers to the Third World 1984-1991*, Congressional Research Service Report for Congress (Washington, D.C.: Congressional Research Service, July 1992), 71, and *Arms Transfers to the Third World 1985-1992*, 58. See also *1991 SIPRI Yearbook*, 209, on trade from 1986 to 1990, which puts Iraqi purchases at triple those of Iran.

[18] From $12.87 billion in 1988 to $4.7 billion in 1990. See *The Military Balance, 1989-90*, 101; *The Military Balance, 1990-91*, 104; *The Military Balance, 1991-92*, 213.

[19] The two forces can be compared in *The Military Balance, 1990-91*, 103-6.

[20] Testimony of Robert Gates, director of the Central Intelligence Agency, before the Defense Policy Panel and the Department of Energy Defense Nuclear Facilities Panel of the House Armed Services Committee, "Regional Threats and Defense Options for the 1990s," March 27, 1992, H.A.S.C. no. 102-73, pp. 313-22. See also Jeffrey Smith, "Gates Warns of Iranian Arms Drive," *Washington Post*, March 28, 1992. The other report was by Barton Gellman, "Iraqi Forces Now Half of Pre-War Power," Defense Intelligence Agency and was summarized in *International Herald Tribune*, August 7, 1992. See also *The Military Balance 1991-92*, 98-101, 107-8.

[21] Defense Intelligence Agency estimate, private communication. July 1993.

[22] I am indebted in the section that follows to Anthony Cordesman's careful and detailed work, especially *After the Storm: The Changing Military Balance in the Middle East* (Boulder, Colo./London: Westview/

Mansell, 1993) 392-416. See also the same author's latest work *Iran and Iraq: The Threat to the Northern Gulf* (Boulder, Colo: Westview Press, forthcoming).

[23] Consisting of forty Su-22's, twenty-four Su-24's, four Su-20's, seven Su-25's, four Mig-29's, seven Mig-23L's, four Mig-23BN's and twenty-four Mirage F-1's.

[24] The Su-24 can carry payloads of 25,000 pounds (11,363 kilograms) for a radius of 1,300 kilometers (780 miles) while carrying 6,500 pounds (2,954 kilograms) of fuel. Cordesman, *After the Storm*, 409.

[25] *Strategic Survey 1991-92* (London: International Institute for Strategic Studies, 1992), 107. While these figures seem high, the essential point is that Iran is building on its acquisitions from Iraq with arms from the former Soviet bloc at a pace that has not been seen since before the revolution.

[26] See especially Jacques Isnard, "Le Rearmement de L'Iran préoccupe les Occidentaux," *Le Monde*, July 25, 1992; Yousseff Ibrahim, "Iran Said to Expropriate 132 Iraqi Planes That Fled War," *International Herald Tribune*, July 31, 1992; Yousseff Ibrahim, "Heavy Arms Outlays Said to Strain Iran," *International Herald Tribune*, August 10, 1992. For a general report see also Scheherazade Daneshkhu, "Iran Presses on with Campaign to Rebuild Its Military Might," *Financial Times*, February 6, 1992.

[27] See R. Mackenzie, "Iran Resurgent," *Air Force Magazine* 75, no. 7 (July 1992): 78-81; Kenneth R. Timmerman, *Weapons of Mass Destruction: The Cases of Iran, Syria and Libya* (Los Angeles: Simon Wiesenthal Center Special Report, August 1992); "Official Iranian Air Force sources...," *Military Technology*, March 1992, 88; Mohammed Ziarati, "Iranian National Security Policy," *Middle East International*, April 3, 1992; Glen Howard and Robert Kramer, "Backfires to Iran: Increased Combat Potential or Headache?" *Notes on Russia and Central Asia* (McLean, Va.: Foreign Systems Research Center, Science Applications International Corporation—SAIC) August 20, 1992. On the question of the TU-22M Backfire see Bill Sweetman, "The Backfire Business: Is Russia Exporting Trouble?" *The Washington Post*, November 29, 1992; Glen Howard and Robert Kramer, "Iran's Quest for Greater Airpower," SAIC Foreign Systems Research Center Analytical Note, A92-049/UL, October 29, 1992; Glen Howard, "Rebuilding the Iranian Airforce," SAIC Foreign Systems Research Cen-

ter Analytical Note, A92-055/UL, December 10, 1992.

[28] *The Military Balance 1992-93*, 103, 109-10.

[29] Matthews interview with Akbar Torkan, *Financial Times*.

[30] Cordesman, *After the Storm*, 408.

[31] Cordesman, *After the Storm*, 410-11.

[32] In addition, Iran wanted to sell back to the United States the seventy-eight F-14 aircraft the Shah bought. See "Proposed Arms Sales for Countries in the Middle East," hearing before the Subcommittee on Europe and the Middle East, 96th Congress, 1st session, August 1, 1979, 32, 34.

[33] Iranian leaders characterize the purchase as a holdover from prerevolutionary days, since orders for the German and U.S. submarines had never been filled. They emphasize that the subs are needed "to fill the gaps in an old military plan" and that without this link "the defensive chain would become weak." Roger Matthews, Akbar Torkan interview; Rear Adm. Abbas Mohtaj, deputy commander of the Navy, Agence France Presse in English (November 30 in ME/1552/A/6, December 1, 1992, and SU/1552/C1/3, December 1, 1992) and Rafsanjani, press conference (January 31, IRNA in ME/1602/A/5, February 2, 1993) and *Vision of IRI* (February 1, ME/1602/A/4, February 4, 1993).

[34] Cordesman, *After the Storm*, 416. Iran already has two or three minisubs from North Korea about which there is little information and has ordered others from Russia.

[35] Cordesman, *After the Storm*, 414.

[36] See Michael Collins Dunn, "Iran's Amphibious Maneuvers Add to Gulf Neighbors' Jitters," *Armed Forces Journal International*, July 1992. For the Victory-4 exercise in April 1993 see *Voice of the IRI* (May 4 in ME/1682/A/7, May 7, 1993).

[37] See testimony of James Woolsey, director of the Central Intelligence Agency, before the Senate Governmental Affairs Committee, February 24, 1993, in which he noted that Iraq still retains an ability to launch

Scud missiles.

[38] See the thoughtful analysis by W. Seth Carus, "Proliferation and Security in Southwest Asia," May 21, 1993, unpublished paper presented at the 1993 U.S. Central Command Southwest Asia Symposium, pp. 6-7, Note also his citation of Russian intelligence's assessment of the bottlenecks in Iran's missile program.

[39] Cordesman, *After the Storm*, 418 (quoting Israeli experts).

[40] See Cordesman, *After the Storm*, 418. For various reports see *Strategic Survey 1988-89*, 15-25; Aaron Karp, "Ballistic Missile Proliferation," *1991 SIPRI Yearbook*, 317-339; Chart entitled Missile Capabilities of Selected Countries, *Missile Monitor* no. 3 (Spring 1993) 1-3; Timothy McCarthy, "Chronology of PRC Missile Trade and Developments" Monterey Institute of International Studies Report, February 1992; and Joseph S. Bermudez, Jr., "Ballistic Missile Development in Iran," paper prepared for the Missile Proliferation Project of the Monterey Institute of International Studies, August 28, 1992.

[41] Chief of the Armed Forces Command Headquarters, Hoseyn Firuzabadi, IRNA in English (March 14 in FBIS-NES-91-051, March 15, 1991, pp. 44-45.

[42] Rafsanjani, press conference, *Voice of the IRI* (February 1 in ME/1603/A/5, February 3, 1993). He also stated: "We do not intend to get access to chemical and nuclear weapons." See IRNA (January 31 in ME/1602/A/5, February 2, 1993).

[43] See excerpts from Foreign Minister Velayati's comments on *Vision of the IRI* (March 18 in ME/0717/A/3, March 20, 1990); and Barry James, "Libyan Fire Throws a Cold Light on Spread of Toxic Arms," *International Herald Tribune*, March 16, 1990.

[44] For Velayati's comments on his contribution to the meeting of the nonaligned movement see *Vision of the IRI* (September 9 in ME/1174/A/5, September 11, 1991). Iran also held up approval of the text at the last minute in order to get a compromise on the membership of the executive council. See "Iran Stalls U.N. Ban on Chemical Weapons," *Financial Times*, September 4, 1992.

[45] The Australia Group consists of major exporters of chemicals that have met biannually since 1985 to define lists of problem substances and technologies, exchange intelligence on problem countries and coordinate export controls with the aim of preventing the spread of chemical and biological weapons.

[46] Reports came from India in mid-1989 and from the United Kingdom in 1990. For the latter see, "India Accused in Poison Gas Role in the Middle East"; Steve Engelberg and Michael Gordon, *The Times* (London), July 11, 1989, Ian Mather and Sebastian Grant, "U.S. Halts British "nerve gas" Plant Deal in Iran," *The Observer* (London), February 4, 1990.

[47] For background on Iran's chemical weapons capabilities see Cordesman, *Weapons of Mass Destruction*, 54, 56.

[48] Testimony to Congress by Robert Gates, director, Central Intelligence Agency, March 27, 1992, in "Regional Threats and Defense Options for the 1990s," hearings before the Defense Policy Panel and the Department of Energy Defense Nuclear Facilities Panel of the House Armed Services Committee, p. 317. See also Elaine Sciolino, "CIA Says Iran Makes Progress on Atom Arms," *New York Times*, November 30, 1992.

[49] See "Global Spread of Chemical and Biological Weapons: Assessing Challenges and Responses," testimony of William H. Webster, director of CIA, in hearings before the Senate Committee on Governmental Affairs," 101st Congress, 1st session, February 9, 1989, pp. 12-13. Webster's successor, Robert Gates, elaborated on this in "Weapons Proliferation: The Most Dangerous Challenge to American Intelligence," (Sacramento, Calif.: Comstock Club, December 15, 1992, mimeo; and George Hardner, Jr., and R. Jeffrey Smith, "CIA Chief Disputing U.N., Warns of Iraqi Nuclear Cache," *International Herald Tribune*, December 19, 1992 (a report based on speeches by Robert Gates). See also Cordesman, *Weapons of Mass Destruction*, 82-84.

[50] See testimony of James Woolsey, director, Central Intelligence Agency, before the Senate Governmental Affairs Committee, February 24, 1993, and before the House Foreign Affairs Committee on International Security, International Organizations and Human Rights ("US Security Policy vis-a-vis Rogue Regimes"), July 28, 1993. Testimony of James Woolsey to Senate Judiciary Committee, "Terrorism in America,"

April 21, 1993.

[51] Cordesman, *After the Storm*, 418-21; Cordesman, *Weapons of Mass Destruction*, 82-84.

[52] Woolsey testimony before the Senate Governmental Affairs Committee, February 24, 1993.

[53] For an excellent general discussion see Brad Roberts, "Chemical Disarmament and International Security," *Adelphi Papers*, no. 267, (London: International Institute for Strategic Security, Spring 1992). See also Roberts "From Nonproliferation to Antiproliferation," *International Security* 18, no. 1 (Summer 1993) 139-73. Roberts develops the concept of "leveraging technologies" (148-49), weapons which can magnify capabilities in an "otherwise unsophisticated force structure." This has direct relevance and application to Iran's case. See also A. F. Mullins, "Weapons of Mass Destruction in the Developing World," unpublished draft paper prepared for the Workshop on Advanced Weapons in the Developing World, American Association for the Advancement of Science, Washington, D.C., June 12, 1992.

[54] In Iran there is little discussion of the utility of nuclear weapons as such; furthermore, it is likely that there are different views on the whole subject of the nuclear energy program. Statements made tend to be general and ambiguous. What follows therefore is an assessment based on analogy, speculation and analysis, derived from patterns of activity and reasoning visible in Iranian statements and conditioned by Iran's world view and the influence of its recent experience.

[55] These views have been voiced on numerous occasions. For statements by the director of Iran's Nuclear Energy Organization, Reza Amrollahi, see IRNA in English (August 3, in ME/1142/A/14, August 5, 1991); IRNA in English (September 1, in ME/W0196/A/1-2, September 10, 1991; September 1 in ME/W0196/A/1-2, September 10, 1991); For press commentary see *Kayhan International* (October 18, 1990 in FBIS-NES-90-203, October 18, 1990); *Voice of the IRI* commentary (July 10 in ME/1122/A/4, July 12, 1991). The Iranian representative to the U.N. Committee on Disarmament made the argument that what appeared to some advanced states to be a security issue was for others a question of access to technology. See *Voice of the IRI*, commentary (August 11 in

ME/1767/A/9, August 14, 1993).

[56] See Reza Amrollahi on "Iran's right," *Voice of the IRI*, (September 17 in ME/W1098/A/2, September 24, 1991); on "generations" see *Voice of the IRI* and IRNA in English (November 6 in ME/1224/A/12-13, November 8, 1991).

[57] See IRNA in English (May 9 in ME/0761/A/2, May 11, 1990). For one example of Vice-President Hassan Habibi's many comments in support of a zone free of weapons of mass destruction, see press conference, *Vision of the IRI* (November 4 in ME/1222/A/12-13, November 6, 1991). Iran does not cite this proposal as Egyptian President Mubarak's initiative. For example see Foreign Minister Velayati's comments to the International Atomic Energy Agency (IAEA) Director-General, Hans Blix, IRNA (November 7 in ME/0916/A/10, November 8, 1991). A discussion of some of the issues and linkages involved that outlines possible approaches to the dilemma is to be found in the excellent report by a group of experts to the secretary-general, *Effective and Verifiable Measures Which Would Facilitate the Establishment of a Nuclear Free Zone in the Middle East* (New York: United Nations Department of Disarmament Affairs, 1991, sales no. E.91. IX.14), For the case of India see the Indian foreign secretary's comments (in ME/1647/i, March 26, 1993) in which he refers to "the general pressure on India for non-proliferation nowadays."

[58] U.S. Secretary of State Baker told a group in 1991 that the Iraqi example showed that even IAEA safeguards "cannot ensure that a renegade regime will not seek to acquire nuclear weapons." Speech to Japan's Institute of International Affairs, Tokyo, November 11, 1991, referenced in a U.S. Embassy "Backgrounder" (Department of Public Affairs), Geneva; for the text, see Federal News Service, November 11-12, 1991. See also Thomas Friedman, "Baker Asks Japan to Broaden Role," *New York Times*, November 12, 1991.

[59] Speech to Air Force pilots (November 17 in ME/1233/A/6-7, November 19, 1991). See also "U.S. Nuclear Technology Tactics Vex Iran," *The New York Times*, November 18, 1991, p. A9. The theme of the United States finding supposed pretexts for technology denial and discrimination is a common one. See *Voice of the IRI* (February 13 in ME/1305/A/6-7, February 15, 1992, 93). U.S. pressure or influence has been brought to bear against Argentina, India, Pakistan and less successfully against China

and Russia. See Cordesman, *Weapons of Mass Destruction*, 105-106; Leonard Spector, "Nuclear Proliferation in the Middle East," *Orbis*, 36, no. 2 (Spring 1992) 187; Parabo, "A Chronology of Iran's Nuclear Program," 58-62; Albright and Hibbs, "Spotlight Shifts," 11. For an official Pakistani denial see Deputy Prime Minister Hosayn Hagani, *Voice of the IRI*, (January 12 in ME/1276/1/7, January 13, 1992). For press reports on these, see "Brazilian Nuclear Deal Now," *Financial Times*, December 5, 1991; *Voice of the IRI* (January 12 in ME/1276/A/7, January 13, 1992); Steve Coll, "Iran Reported Trying to Buy Indian Reactor," *Washington Post*, November 15, 1991; and "India Withdraws Offer to Iran of Nuclear Reactor," *Financial Times*, November 21, 1991; "L'Argentine Entreprend la Livraison de Matérial Nucléaire a L'Iran," *Le Monde*, January 29, 1992.

[60] See respectively, Majlis Speaker Nateq Nouri, IRNA in English (June 8 in ME/1711/A/9, June 10, 1993); Reza Amrollahi, *Voice of the IRI* (March 15 in ME/1637/A/6, March 15, 1993).

[61] *Voice of the IRI* (December 1, in ME/1555/A/6, December 4, 1992).

[62] For one example see the remarks of the Israeli Air Force commander, Herzl Bodinger, *IDF Radio*, Tel Aviv (June 14 in ME/1408/A/8-9, June 16, 1992). For texts, see *Voice of the IRI* (July 8 in ME/1429/A/9, July 10, 1992); and *Voice of the IRI* (July 14 in ME/1433/A/15, July 15, 1992). The latter accused Israel of "overtly following an aggressive nuclear policy" and of constituting "the greatest danger to regional and international peace."

[63] For a summary see Leonard Spector, *Nuclear Ambitions: The Spread of Nuclear Weapons 1989-90*, (Boulder, Colo.: Westview Press [in association with the Carnegie Endowment for International Peace], 1990) chapter 12, 203-18; Spector, "Nuclear Proliferation in the Middle East," 181-98; Cordesman, *Weapons of Mass Destruction*, 103-6; Akbar Etemad, "Iran," chapter 7 in Harald Muller, ed., *A European Non-Proliferation Policy: Prospects and Problems*, (Oxford: Clarendon Press, 1987), 203-27.

[64] These figures are taken from those offered by Reza Amrollahi, *Voice of the IRI* ("call-in" program), (August 13 in ME/1460/A/3-4, August 15, 1992); and Amrollahi in IRNA (Vienna) in English (February 26 in ME/1316/A/9, February 28, 1992). On a new purchase from China see, "China Offers A-Plants to Egypt and Others," *International Herald Tribune*, July 31, 1992; Yvonne Preston, "Rafsanjani China Visit Raises Nu-

clear Arms Fears," *Financial Times*, September 10, 1992; Elaine Sciolino, "China Will Build A-Plant for Iran," *New York Times*, September 11, 1992, p. A6; J. P. Perrin, "Chine-Iran: Coopération Nucléaire," *Liberation* (Paris), September 14, 1992. An agreement on completion of one 300-megawatt reactor (rather than two) was finalized in July 1993.

[65] Gordon Oehler, director of the CIA Nuclear Proliferation Center, "U.S. Security Policy vis-à-vis Rogue States," testimony before the House Foreign Affairs Committee, July 28, 1993. See also Leonard Spector, "Is Iran Building a Bomb?" *Christian Science Monitor*, December 31, 1991; Jeffrey Smith, "U.S. Worry: Nuclear Aid by Beijing to Tehran," *International Herald Tribune*, October 31, 1991; David Albright and Mark Hibbs, "Spotlight Shifts to Iran," *Bulletin of Atomic Scientists*, March 1992, 9-11; Jim Mann, "U.S. Suspects China Aids Iran on Arms," *International Herald Tribune*, March 18, 1992, 5. Betsy Parabo, "A Chronology of Iran's Nuclear Program," *Eye on Supply*, Monterey Institute of International Studies, Emerging Nuclear Suppliers Project, No. 7, Fall 1992, 45-71.

[66] Some careful analysts doubt that Iran is able to mount an indigenous program within ten years as much for organizational and financial reasons as for technological ones. See especially W. Seth Carus, "Proliferation and Security in Southwest Asia." He cites a study by the Intelligence Department of the Russian Federation that shares his skepticism, even given an annual investment of between $1 billion and $1.5 billion and outside assistance. It is worth summarizing the three paths to a nuclear bomb: individual; in cooperation with other regional states; in cooperation with friendly suppliers. There are difficulties with each since all major suppliers are now party to the NPT and its strict full-scope safeguards; and regional partners are either more advanced (Pakistan) and sensitive to sanctions, more backward (Libya), or truly isolated and under surveillance (North Korea).

[67] The economics of nuclear power plants and the decline in oil prices no longer justify (if they ever did) the idea that Iran could use nuclear power more cheaply while relying on oil (and oil products) to export for income. Thus, the justification for the Shah's nuclear program no longer exists. Moreover, Iran lies in an earthquake zone, and the war with Iraq demonstrated that adversaries were willing to target nuclear installations. Both are reasons for increasing skepticism about the need for nuclear power.

[68] Tehran, domestic service, November 6 in FBIS-NES-90-216, 50-1, November 7, 1990.

[69] See *Kayhan International*, editorial, "Work on an Alternative" (July 7 in FBIS-NES-93-136, pp. 74-75, July 19, 1993).

[70] Vice-President Attollah Mojaherani in *Abrar* (an Iranian newspaper); interview cited on Radio Moscow in Persian (November 2 in SU/1221/A4/2, November 5, 1991); and Ayatollah Meshkini, speaker of the Assembly of Experts, in a sermon, *Vision of the IRI* (December 6 in ME/1250/A/10-11, December 9, 1991).

[71] Maj. Gen. Ali Shahbazi, *Voice of the IRI* (November 19 in ME/1234/A/7, November 20, 1991). Air Force Commander Brig. Gen. Mansur Sattari has insisted that Iran's nuclear program is peaceful and allegations to the contrary are "completely baseless," IRNA (June 17; in ME/1412/A/10, June 20, 1992).

[72] Khamenei to Basij commanders, *Voice of the IRI* (July 13 in ME/1433/A/13-14, July 15, 1992). Note also Foreign Minister Velayati's categorical denial of any intention to acquire or develop nuclear, chemical or biological weapons, *Voice of the IRI* in English (August 1 in ME/1449/A/13, August 3, 1992). Reza Amrollahi echoes Khamenei's thought that nuclear weapons do not confer power on their possessor and cites the example of the former USSR. See *Voice of the IRI* (March 13 in ME/1637/A/6, March 15, 1993).

[73] Rafsanjani told Air Force Academy graduates that the war with Iraq clearly showed that safeguarding independence and existence under inhospitable international conditions is not possible without science and equipment" (November 17 in ME/1233/A/6-7, November 19, 1991). See also, *Voice of the IRI* (February 10 in ME/1301/A/7, February 11, 1992).

IMPACT ON REGIONAL AND INTERNATIONAL SECURITY

[1] Deputy Foreign Minister Ahmed Besharati, IRI, Tehran, (November 21 in ME/0621/A/1-2, November 23, 1989).

[2] Hence the Gulf Cooperation Council's and Arab League's reaction to Iran's restrictions on Sharjah's administration of Abu Musa in 1992, basi-

cally that Iran was annexing the island. Iran, which disputes the current shared sovereignty of the island with Sharjah, never denounced the 1971 agreement governing administration or made any new claim to the island. The subject is under discussion.

[3] W. Seth Carus, *Ballistic Missiles in the Third World: Threat and Response* (New York: Praeger, 1990) 32. (Published in cooperation with the Center for Strategic and International Studies, Washington, D.C.)

[4] W. Seth Carus and Joseph Bermudez, "Iran's Growing Missile Forces," 131; quoted in Martin Navias, "Ballistic Missile Proliferation in the Middle East," *Survival* 31, no. 3 (May-June 1989): 232. By comparison, consider that Saudi Arabia's missile force, equipped with 2,000-kilogram explosives could "deliver 240 tons, six times as much explosive as Iraqi missiles dropped on Tehran during the war of the cities. See Karp, "Ballistic Missile Proliferation," *1991 SIPRI Yearbook*, 325.

[5] See Martin Navias, "Ballistic Missile Proliferation."

[6] See Karl Kaiser, "Nonproliferation and Nuclear Deterrence," *Survival* 31, no. 2 (March-April 1989): 131.

[7] This seems to be the assessment of some intelligence estimates that assume Iran's capacity to dominate the Persian Gulf by the end of the decade. See Sciolino, "CIA Says Iran Makes Progress on Atom Arms."

[8] John J. Fialka, "Iran's New Submarine, Built by Russia, Stirs, Concern in the U.S. Navy," *Wall Street Journal*, November 16, 1992.

[9] Once Iran receives all three Kilo-class submarines in 1994, and assuming it has a moderately trained crew of fifty or more men per submarine ready for operations, a number of problems remain. The Gulf's waters are too shallow to be practical for submarine operations. Basing the submarines inside the Gulf would risk bottling them up. Basing them outside at Chah Behar on the Gulf of Oman requires completion of a base whose construction was first planned by the Shah in the mid-1970s.

With three submarines, only one would be operational at any one time. Without experience it will be some time before they will be deployed with any great effect. They will in addition remain vulnerable insofar as their base can always be hit even if their actual location at any one time may be uncertain.

Practically, their chief role would be to lay mines and deter external forces from entering the Gulf's waters. Within the Gulf, they may impress the smaller Gulf states, some of which (the UAE, for example) are already looking for antisubmarine warfare capabilities. Their use or utility short of actual warfare is limited and even in the case of conflict, their value given their cost remains questionable.

[10] As the technology for precision guidance of cruise missiles becomes more widely available through the general introduction of satellite navigation systems, antiship cruise missiles could become a threat in the Persian Gulf, especially if they resist jamming or countermeasures. Such advances would compound the difficulty of U.S. sea control. See John Roche, "Tactical Aircraft, Ballistic Missiles and Cruise Missile Proliferation in the Developing World," unpublished draft paper prepared for the Workshop on Advanced Weapons in the Developing World, American Association for the Advancement of Science, Washington, D.C., June 12, 1992, 9-11.

[11] To take just three instances: Defense Ministry Director Gen. David Ivri: "Iranian weapons procurement threatens to kindle conflicts in the Middle East..." *IDF Radio*, Tel Aviv (June 5 in ME/1093/A/11-12, June 8, 1991); Maj. Gen. Uri Sagi, head of the intelligence branch, says that Iran is conducting a very worrying nuclear project and will be capable of reaching independent nuclear capability by the end of the decade, *IDF Radio*, Tel Aviv, (June 8 in ME/1403/A/5, June 10, 1992); off-the-record remarks by Israeli military officials expressing concern about Iran's nuclear plans and conventional arms acquisitions are found in Hugh Carnegy, "Israel Worried Over Iran's Nuclear Plans," *Financial Times*, January 29, 1992.

[12] See Deputy Defense Minister Mordechai Gur on the difference between deterring Iraq and Syria. "Iraq could attack us with missiles. Since we do not share a border, we could not put to use the IDF's full deterrent power. However, that is not the case when it comes to the Syrians. In other words, the Syrians must take into account that the moment they fire a missile we may start marching on Damascus." Thus in theory, Iran, like Iraq is not so readily deterred. The same considerations hold true of its defense against Iran. Israel Broadcasting Authority Television, Jerusalem (August 13 in ME/1460/A/6, August 15, 1992).

[13] Note Rabin's reference to this in his address to the Knesset: "The possibility that nuclear weapons may make their appearance in the Middle East in the next few years is a negative and very serious development from Israel's point of view." Israel Broadcasting Authority Television, Jerusalem (July 13 in ME/1433/A/3, July 15, 1992). See also Gideon Rafael "Israel Has Opened a Window, Rabin is Gauging the Winds," *International Herald Tribune*, August 3, 1992. Shimon Peres, Israel's foreign minister, has referred to the strategic linkages forged by long-range weapons: "We have to face the new technologies and processes in the world. We cannot run away from them. The range of a missile forces us to have regional security." *MacNeil/Lehrer NewsHour*, September 23, 1992, as cited in "For the Record" The *Washington Post*, September 25, 1992. Quoted in Roberts "From Nonproliferation to Antiproliferaton," 157, note 63.

DECISIONMAKING AND NATIONAL SECURITY

[1] Rafsanjani, *Voice of the IRI* (February 11 in ME/1303/A/3, February 13, 1992). Note also Spiritual Leader Khamenei's argument that Algeria's move toward Islam proved "the righteousness of the Islamic claim of the resisting and pioneering Iranian nation," in remarks made in Bushire (January 1 in ME/1269/A/3, January 4, 1992).

[2] "Is it fair then that we should say something against such a regime as ours?" *Voice of the IRI* (May 28 in ME/1354/A/7, May 30, 1992).

[3] Press conference (January 31 in ME/1604/A/16, February 4, 1993).

[4] Contrast for example Rafsanjani's pronouncements on economic issues with the fire-and-brimstone statement of Ayatollah Abdolkarim Musavi-Ardebili, member of the Assembly for the Discernment of What is Best: Rafsanjani stresses the need for development and the dangers of economic failure for the revolution by analogy with the failure of most recent revolutions. Musavi-Ardebili argues that Iran does not want to be another Japan: "If today in a miraculous way we become a Japan, can we claim to have reached our objectives? It was not the objective of the revolution to become like some countries which have a strong and sound economy, a strong currency and a high standard of living.... The objectives of the revolution were far superior to these.... The will to court martyrdom and self-denial has enabled us today to be the owner of a revolution, the kind of revolution, which

is Islamic and in which we can take pride. It is unique in the world.... It was the revolution... and its export, which revived Islam and Islamic thought in Egypt. It has brought Algeria, Morocco and Somalia to their present situation. How did the revolution do so? By the blessing of the blood of its martyrs...." Friday sermon, Tehran University, *Voice of the IRI* (August 27 in ME/1780/MED/16-17, August 30, 1993). For Rafsanjani's remarks see Tehran domestic service (May 28 in FBIS-NES-90-105, May 31, 1990).

[5] On both the question of ending the war with Iraq and of succession, Khomeinei's followers sought to get his decision, aware of the dangers of a power struggle. Rafsanjani later said Khomeini "did not consider it advisable that the war go on in our country after him...[and] "if the Imam had not solved the question of leadership ... we would have faced difficulties after his demise" (speaking near the anniversary of Ayatollah Khomeini's death, Tehran IRI (May 31 in ME/0780/i, June 2, 1990).

[6] The discussion that follows is based on the author's interviews with Iranian diplomats and officials in 1992-93.

[7] Changes are possible but only in the wake of crises, which provide a cover or a diversion. Hence Iran resumed relations with Saudi Arabia in April 1991 despite the express prohibition of this in Khomeini's will. Iran's leaders did so in part because of the political costs of not having access to the Hadj (the pilgrimage to Mecca for Iran's Muslims).

[8] See Chubin and Tripp, *Iran and Iraq at War.*

[9] Witness Iran's initial opposition to the 1989 Taif agreement which set it on a collision course with Syria in Lebanon. Tehran reversed course quickly.

CONCLUSIONS

[1] Iran has had its balance of payments in the red for ten of the past fourteen years, a budget deficit every year for fourteen years, unemployment of 15 to 30 percent and inflation of 20 to 40 percent. GNP in 1991-92 allowing for inflation was close to that of 1978-79. GDP levels were the same. Given population growth of some 40 percent in the period, GNP per capita has plunged by as much as 50 percent. For an overview see Jahangir Amuzegar "The Iranian Economy before and after the Revolution," *The Middle East Journal* 46, no. 3, (Summer 1992): 413-15; Patrick Clawson, "Economic

Development in the Persian Gulf in the Face of Low Oil Income," *The Iranian Journal of International Affairs* 2, no. 1 (Spring 1990): 188.

[2] Rafsanjani noted in 1991: "We have a lot of work that we did not touch because of the war. This is the most expensive and hidden cost no one takes into account...We did not build dams, so we are facing a lack of water. We did not build refineries, so we have to import oil now...We did not allocate enough for agriculture." Rafsanjani sermon, *Voice of the IRI*, May 24 in ME/1082/A/3, May 27, 1991.

[3] See Errand Abrahamian, *Khomeinism*, Berkeley: University of California Press (1993).